Thinking Together

9 Beliefs for Building a Mathematical Community

Rozlynn Dance and **Tessa Kaplan**

HEINEMANN
Portsmouth, NH

Heinemann
361 Hanover Street
Portsmouth, NH 03801–3912
www.heinemann.com

Offices and agents throughout the world

The authors and publisher wish to thank those who have generously given permission to reprint borrowed material:

Eight principles of effective instruction from *Principles to Actions: Ensuring Mathematical Success for All* by National Council of Teachers of Mathematics (NCTM). Copyright © 2014 by NCTM. Published by NCTM, Reston, VA. Reprinted by permission of the publisher, conveyed through Copyright Clearance Center, Inc.

Library of Congress Cataloging-in-Publication Data
Names: Dance, Rozlynn, author. | Kaplan, Tessa, author.
Title: Thinking together : 9 beliefs for building a mathematical community / Rozlynn Dance and Tessa Kaplan.
Description: Portsmouth, NH : Heinemann, [2018] | Includes bibliographical references.
Identifiers: LCCN 2017045594 | ISBN 9780325098180
Subjects: LCSH: Mathematics teachers—Training of. | Mathematics—Study and teaching (Elementary). | Elementary school teachers—Training of. | Effective teaching.
Classification: LCC QA10.5 .K37 2018 | DDC 372.7/044—dc23
LC record available at https://lccn.loc.gov/2017045594

Editor: Katherine Bryant
Production: Victoria Merecki
Cover design: Suzanne Heiser
Text design: Sue Godel
Typesetter: Kim Arney
Cover photo: © Getty Images/FatCamera
Author photos: Tami Baumgartner Photography
Manufacturing: Steve Bernier

Printed in the United States of America on acid-free paper
22 21 20 19 18 RWP 1 2 3 4 5

Contents

Foreword

The members of my family have varied relationships with math. My wife Bridget loves math and even today enjoys figuring out challenging math problems when helping our high school-age children with math. I'm not as confident with math, so I'm happy to let her handle math homework (not that I'd be much help), but I absolutely loved teaching math as a first-grade teacher. Our son Harrison is an actuary, and his whole work life is high-level math. Our daughters Meredith and Molly have both positive and negative feelings toward math that haven't shifted as much over time. But it is our daughter Natalie who has the most tenuous relationship with math. Some years she loves math and feels confident. Other years she dislikes math, and you can see her confidence wane.

Natalie's a fairly introspective fourteen-year-old, so I asked her to talk about what affected her feelings toward math from year to year. She quickly rattled off the influences on her mathematical confidence.

- She talked about the positive impact of *low-pressure* opportunities to solve mathematical problems with *guided support* from the teacher.
- She said it was easier to *form questions* when you are actually solving a problem, and much harder to form questions when listening to a lesson.
- She mentioned the importance of frequent *feedback* at school, rather than trying to figure it out on your own at home (and stressing about whether it was right).
- She said her favorite years were those where the focus was on *understanding* mathematical ideas (process) as opposed to getting answers correct (product).
- She said that *exploring and doing* was a better way of transferring understanding than telling and explaining.

The years where teachers made classroom decisions that supported these ideas, Natalie flourished.

Simply put, the decisions teachers make matter and have lasting effects. Throughout this book, Rozlynn Dance and Tessa Kaplan provide specific strategies that will help *you* make decisions that benefit all of the learners in your class.

You're about to read a math book that isn't only about math. It's really a book about the conditions that maximize learning for any child in any content area. Just to prove this, I read a whole chapter and each time I came to the word *math*, I skipped it. The meaning of the sentence didn't change. Good teaching, no matter the subject, is rooted in fundamentally similar key practices, which form the foundation for this book. Much of the professional work I do is in writing, and I was continually struck by the parallels to writing instruction as I read this book. For example, in writing we think about the importance of composition, the ability to create meaning on a page, in addition to conventions (spelling, punctuation, etc.). The authors talk about the important role of sense making in math (Chapter 4) and how understanding is the goal, in addition to being able to solve problems. In math as in writing we want children to have a sense of ownership and control, whether it's deciding on a strategy to solve a math problem or deciding which strategy to use to convey feelings in a piece of writing.

But, it's important that the focus of this book is on math, because so many children (and teachers) lack confidence in math. Students and adults often feel that their disposition toward math is set, thinking that they are either good at math or not good at math. Rozlynn and Tessa show us that isn't true. They show us strategies teachers can use that will help improve children's disposition toward math and solving problems (and other content areas as well). And those dispositions are critical. Lilian Katz defines a disposition as "a pattern of behavior exhibited frequently and in the absence of coercion and constituting a habit of mind under some conscious and voluntary control, and that it is intentional and oriented towards broad goals" (Katz 1993). Although it is possible to learn despite a negative disposition toward what you are learning, learning is more efficient, lasting, and enjoyable when the learner has a positive disposition toward the learning, especially math.

By focusing on dispositions and key principles about learning math, Rozlynn and Tessa provide teachers and students with ideas and skills that will last long beyond the school year. Just to be sure, I ran some of these ideas by my son Harrison. As an actuary, he spends his days doing high-level math related to probability. To become a fully certified actuary you have to take a series of exams over the course of many years. So, I asked him, to pass these exams, isn't it all about getting the right answer and knowing how to solve the algorithms? He told me that although he certainly has to know formulas and algorithms, that wasn't enough. He said that to solve the problems he encounters, he has to be able to *understand the process and theory* and decide how to solve it. Even at a high level, there are *multiple strategies* to get to an answer, but to consider and use multiple strategies you have to truly understand the process. The ideas of multiple pathways to solve a problem, mistakes as opportunities for learning, and the importance of understanding permeate this book. Both first graders and actuaries need to be able to do more than solve an algorithm. They have to be able to play with ideas, consider multiple possibilities, and apply what they know to new situations.

Throughout the book, Rozlynn and Tessa are respectful of children and childhood. They embed their decisions in what they know is right for children based on who they are right now. That sounds obvious, but actually isn't easy in the "pushdown" world of education, where, in a race to always go further faster, depth and understanding are pushed aside. Rozlynn and Tessa make the case for pushing from the ground up and providing children with the skills, strategies, and dispositions that they need now *and* going forward.

The authors also support positive dispositions toward math for teachers, by thinking about adult learning in the same way as they do student learning, and with the same respect for a community of learners. Just as they value mistakes as opportunities for learning, they anticipate that teachers will encounter challenges along the way. In each chapter, you will find a section called "When Things Don't Seem to Be Working." These sections provide valuable, practical tips for what to do when the inevitable happens and our teaching doesn't go as planned. But, more importantly, these sections reflect the belief of the authors that things won't always go smoothly, whether as a teacher or student, and that's OK. They anticipate and celebrate struggles as opportunities for learning.

All children deserve to be in a classroom that nurtures their identities as mathematicians, writers, and readers. To have a positive mathematical identity, all children have to willingly and enthusiastically engage in mathematical thinking each day. Teachers, and the decisions they make, significantly impact children's disposition and identity whether they realize it or not. This book supports your ability to create classroom communities that nurture all children as thinkers.

Acknowledgments

We would like to thank all the teachers and colleagues whom we have worked with throughout the years in Federal Way, Washington; Shoreline, Washington; and Brooklyn, New York. It is through collaboration and problem-solving together that we have been able to improve our own teaching and develop many of the strategies we talk about in this book.

We thank Shirley Mitchell, our math coach, who inspired us and worked closely with us to change our math instruction. Her expertise in teaching intermediate math and her bravery in entering our primary classrooms to figure out how to make it all work kept us thinking reflectively over the years. Whenever we question our instructional choices, we still ask to this day, "What would Shirley do?"

We appreciate the freedom that our principal, Sarah Gill, allowed us to take control of our instructional choices in our classrooms. She trusted us and believed in us when we decided our math instruction needed an overhaul.

We'd also like to thank the Heinemann team for taking a chance on us as new writers. Their incredible support throughout the publishing process has been invaluable. We'd especially like to thank Katherine Bryant, who worked with us for two years, helping us develop this book into what it's become today.

Finally, we thank the children who have inspired us over our years of teaching. Their incredible ability to grow and learn is at the root of every choice we make as they surprise us daily with their creative thinking and reasoning skills. They inspire us to continue to be better teachers. This book is for those children, who deserve the chance to deeply understand and grow to love mathematics.

Chapter One Creating a Community of Mathematicians

As elementary school teachers, we have watched math instruction change and grow drastically during our careers. When we first started teaching math to young children, we taught the way we had been taught as children ourselves. The teacher introduced a new topic or idea, directly showed the students how to do it, and then the students practiced that idea by repeating problem after problem on a worksheet or from a textbook.

In our early years of teaching, however, we started to notice something. After teaching a topic and having our students complete practice problems correctly, we assessed them and most could score well on a test. Yet two to three weeks down the road, when we reviewed or touched on that topic again, our students seemed to have forgotten everything! The problem was this: most of our children could memorize and follow procedures long enough to pass a test, but the minute the knowledge was no longer at the front of their minds, it slipped away. Students weren't deeply understanding and internalizing math concepts; they were just getting by. They were never asked to grapple with complex topics and find solutions to problems on their own. They were never asked to understand why a procedure works; they simply carried out the procedure to get to an answer.

We became unsatisfied with our math instruction and sought to change it. We wanted the students, not the teachers, to be at the center of math learning. We wanted students to learn how to be problem solvers, trying different strategies and persevering until they came to a conclusion. We wanted our students to construct their own knowledge instead of acting as receptacles as we dumped knowledge upon them.

Through collaboration with colleagues and work with an instructional coach who was integral to our growth as teachers, we slowly changed our beliefs about mathematics instruction. The more we read, the more we realized that research supported our changing beliefs, too. In *Principles to Actions,* the authors identify several characteristics of math instruction that promote deep mathematical learning for children. Students must engage with challenging tasks, make connections to what they already know, develop both conceptual and procedural knowledge, construct knowledge through discourse, receive productive feedback, and develop awareness of themselves as learners (NCTM 2014).

Qualities of Effective Mathematics Instruction

Over the years, we learned that in order for students to truly learn and understand mathematical concepts, they must live in classrooms that support cooperative learning and mathematical discourse. They must learn to persevere and focus on the process of math, not the product. And most importantly, they need to construct their own knowledge of mathematics from the ground up in an atmosphere where they feel safe to learn, take risks, make mistakes, and grow.

A SAFE SPACE

In Ms. Kaplan's first-grade classroom, she has just introduced the day's math problem: "Gabriella was helping her mom plant her garden over the weekend. They planted 35 pea seeds. They also planted 54 pumpkin seeds. How many seeds did they plant altogether?" The students have discussed the problem to ensure they understand what they are being asked to do and are released to begin problem-solving.

As soon as the children receive their papers, which are blank except for the day's problem written at the very top, they head back to their seats, pulling out their pencils. Some stop at the math center on their way to their tables, pulling out base ten blocks, connecting cubes, or ten frame mats. When the students are settled with their supplies, a quiet buzz falls over the room as they get to work.

Leo is drawing tally marks. Ashlyn is pulling out tens blocks, quietly asking herself, "How many tens are there?" Some students are drawing ten frames and filling them with circles on their papers. Others are drawing tens and ones mats, making sticks and dots for tens and ones. Some are writing equations and sentences that explain their thinking. A few haven't touched their papers yet and are busy counting connecting cubes or base ten blocks. The students are engaged in solving a problem they haven't been taught how to solve, using tools and strategies that make sense to them.

Students in Ms. Kaplan's class feel safe making their own choices. They try out strategies even when they aren't sure if they'll work, and when they don't work, they try to solve the problem again or give it a go with a different strategy. Beyond that, they trust that their teacher won't be upset if they get the answer wrong or don't finish right away. They trust that their classmates won't make fun of them when they make mistakes but will celebrate them for those mistakes that create new learning. Creating respect between and among the students as well as the teacher in a classroom is the first major building block in creating a classroom community where students can deeply learn math.

CONSTRUCTING KNOWLEDGE

The goal of mathematics instruction in our classrooms is to teach for understanding. In order for students to deeply understand math, they must construct their own knowledge, connecting new ideas with their prior knowledge. Truly developing mathematical concepts means intricately weaving what students know with what they are learning, then looping back repeatedly to deepen and strengthen those connections. According to John A. Van de Walle et al. (2014, 4), "At the heart of constructivism is the notion that learners are not blank slates but rather creators (constructors) of their own learning. All people, all the time, construct or give meaning to things they think about or perceive." When we tell students what to think or how to do math, we take from them the chance to construct their own understanding.

Listen in as Ms. Kaplan talks with Katie, who is struggling to start the problem about Gabriella and her garden. Katie is using base ten blocks to model the first number in the problem, 35.

> **Ms. Kaplan:** *How many do you have here?*
>
> **Katie:** *10, 20, 30, 40 . . . oh wait.* [slowing down, pointing to each ten stick] 10, 20, 30. [picking up one ten stick] *But the 20 is in here.*
>
> **Ms. Kaplan:** *The 20 is in here? . . . 10, 20, 30? What number are we trying to make here?*
>
> **Katie:** [looks at the problem on her paper and points] *35.*
>
> **Ms. Kaplan:** *35, okay. If we have 30 here, what do we need now?*
>
> **Katie:** *One more?*
>
> **Ms. Kaplan:** *Let's try that and see if it works.*

Katie pulls out a single one block. She and Ms. Kaplan count together and find that she now has 31. Through some more trial and error, Katie eventually concludes that she needs 5 more.

In this vignette, Katie is still learning about basic place value concepts. In order to help Katie develop a model of the number 35, Ms. Kaplan acknowledges where she is in her understanding and guides her through questioning toward a deeper understanding. She encourages her to try out ideas and test them to see if they work. Katie is not following the steps in a procedure but persevering through this task as she tries to figure out how to accurately model her thinking.

We can help our students construct their own understanding by teaching them not to rely on the teacher for the answer. We want our students to look within themselves for connections that might help them construct understanding or to talk with their classmates to formulate ideas. We want them to confirm and justify their own thinking. As teachers, we act as facilitators and learning coaches. The teacher is not the source of knowledge but merely a guide on the path toward knowledge construction.

PERSEVERANCE

We also believe that one of the most important factors in successful student-centered instruction and learning is perseverance. For students to be successful mathematicians, they must be willing to struggle through mistakes, take risks in their learning, and try again when things don't quite work out. In his 2010 TED Talk, Dan Meyer discusses the importance of helping our students learn to be patient problem solvers. Children of the twenty-first century are used to quick problems with easy solutions, but real mathematical problems don't work out that way. We need to teach our children to tackle complex problems worth solving and persevere in solving them (Meyer 2010).

According to Jo Boaler (2016, 13), "Studies of successful and unsuccessful business people show . . . what separates the more successful people from the less successful people is not the number of their successes but the number of mistakes they make, with the more successful people making *more* mistakes." When we teach students that mistakes not only are okay but are steps on the path to success and innovation, we help build perseverance. As mathematicians, we want our students to be able to try different paths to a solution, to experiment with new strategies, and to keep trying until they find an idea that works.

We believe that if we let our students give up after the first try or get overly frustrated when they make a mistake, we are doing them a great disservice. The same goes for when we dive in to save them, correcting their thinking or giving them the answer. We are not doing them any favors by bailing them out when they are struggling. The structures we set up in our classroom and the community we build can support our students as they persevere through productive struggle, encouraging them to continue to persist when things get tough.

COOPERATIVE LEARNING AND MATHEMATICAL DISCOURSE

To understand the importance of mathematical discourse, let's step back into Ms. Kaplan's room. The students have finished working on their problem and are gathered on the carpet listening to Harper share how she solved it.

> **Harper:** *My sentence was "I knew that 5 + 4 was the same as 9 and I knew that 30 + 50 was the same as 80. So I put them together and it made 89."*
>
> **Ms. Kaplan:** *Okay, turn to your neighbor and tell them what Harper's sentences mean.*

As Ms. Kaplan listens in on the partner conversations, she can see some confusion about Harper's thinking. Some students are unclear where her numbers came from. Once students turn back to the whole group, Ms. Kaplan begins facilitating a discussion of these ideas. The students work out together, with guiding questions from the teacher, that the 5 and the 4 are the ones in the problem and the 30 and the 50 are the tens. At the end of the discussion, Elliot comments, "I was confused at first, and then when I started talking to Amity . . . um . . . when she was going to talk, I . . . I knew what she meant."

By asking students first to turn and talk about Harper's thinking and then to discuss her thinking as a whole group, Ms. Kaplan was able to guide students toward understanding Harper's mathematical ideas. Students made connections between their own thinking and Harper's thinking, deepening their understanding. Elliot was even able to articulate how helpful it was to be able to hear another student explain Harper's thinking in a different way.

In order to construct knowledge and deepen understanding, students must be able to talk about their learning and understand the ideas of others. The Common Core Standards for Mathematical Practice (CCSSO 2010) specify that students should be able to "construct viable arguments and critique the reasoning of others." When students can justify their own thinking and explain their ideas to their classmates, they are deepening their own understanding of those concepts. When they can critique the reasoning of others, students show that they are thinking deeply about mathematical ideas, making connections between their own thinking and the ideas of others.

On a more complex level, students must not only be able to talk to and listen to one another but also be able to work cooperatively in partners and groups. They must find and build upon the strengths of others, which in turn strengthens their own skills and understanding. Students need the skills to be able to work with one another as they think creatively and problem-solve together. It is our job as teachers to ensure equity of voice among all our students, regardless of skill level or ability. We know that when we encourage cooperative learning, there is a tendency for some students to dominate the discussion. Therefore, to be effective teachers, we must have a variety of techniques on hand to encourage all students to contribute to a discussion (Danielson 2014). Developing those skills requires deliberate and clear structures to be in place in the classroom.

LETTING STUDENTS DO THE THINKING

The study of mathematics is not just about finding answers but about figuring out ways to solve complex problems successfully. Simply put, the process is more important than the product. Because of this, it is important that students take ownership of their learning process as the teacher steps back from being the center of knowledge. During Ms. Kaplan's lesson, three students share their thinking, justify their answer, and answer questions from their classmates about how they found their answer. Not one student ever asks Ms. Kaplan if 89 is actually the correct answer. By talking about and analyzing student strategies for solving the problem, the children come to trust that 89 is the answer without needing confirmation from the teacher.

When students learn to think metacognitively about their own processes by comparing, critiquing, and justifying them, they begin to trust themselves as learners. They don't need an answer key in the back of the book because they have chosen and used strategies that make sense to them. They have checked their answers on their own using different strategies and critiqued their answers to be sure they are reasonable in the context

of the problem. When students are mo ... the correct
answers come more naturally and fluidl

Key Beliefs That Suppor
Effective Mathematics I

In our first few years of teaching, we sp
ics instruction *shouldn't* be. The more c
that mathematics instruction *should* be
identifies eight key principles of effect

1. *Establish mathematics goa*
2. *Implement tasks that prom*
3. *Use and connect mathematical represen*
4. *Facilitate meaningful mathematical discourse.*
5. *Pose purposeful questions.*
6. *Build procedural fluency from conceptual understanding.*
7. *Support productive struggle in learning mathematics.*
8. *Elicit and use evidence of student thinking. (NCTM 2014, 10)*

These eight brief sentences seem simple yet are incredibly complex and daunting. Each of the eight principles, to be adequately implemented in elementary classrooms, must be thought about and planned strategically. Daily, we must ask ourselves:

- Is my task challenging enough, and does it meet my mathematical goal?
- How will I facilitate the connection between mathematical ideas and representations?
- What questions will I ask or encourage my students to ask?
- How will I support students in building their conceptual understanding as they struggle through a task?
- How will my students justify and share their thinking?

After years of teaching through problem-solving-based, student-centered methods, we have realized that there is one common thread that underlies success in all these tasks. As teachers, we must cultivate the structures and beliefs in a classroom community that lay the foundation for the mathematical growth of our students. We must create a kind, caring, trusting community of learners who feel comfortable tackling the unknown, taking risks, and making mistakes. Our foundation is built on a set of nine key beliefs:

1. *Everyone has the right to learn.*
2. *We respect the ideas of others.*
3. *Challenging problems help our brains grow stronger.*
4. *Mistakes are great!*
5. *Good mathematicians are brave and try new things.*
6. *There are different strategies for solving a problem.*
7. *It's not just about the answer.*
8. *Good learners ask questions.*
9. *Questions from the teacher help us learn and grow.*

In this book, we hope to share with you some of the strategies we've learned and developed over the years to help reinforce these beliefs and build the foundation for successful mathematical learning.

In Chapter 2, we will discuss beliefs 1 and 2, sharing strategies for creating a respectful community of learners who believe that everyone has the right to learn. We will also share some strategies to help students understand how to respect the ideas of others as they learn to listen to and critique their classmates' thinking. We'll discuss the importance of honoring mistakes (which we'll return to in Chapter 3), respectfully disagreeing, and giving everyone the time they need to think and learn.

Beliefs 3, 4, and 5 will be the subject of Chapter 3, as we share strategies for building up our students' mathematical confidence. We'll share some ways to build perseverance, set up a structure for sharing and celebrating mistakes, and encourage students to take risks and try new things.

honoring different mathematical strat- 's 6 and 7. We'll share some important nultiple strategies for solving a problem, strategies with the class. We'll also pro- dents justify their thinking.

f questioning, both from the teacher and Ve'll clarify the difference between ques- ide, challenge, and extend; and questions ide some concrete strategies for teaching

s and ideas to help you keep up the momen- tum as y ction so it aligns with these beliefs.

Our goal is to provide you with lessons, ideas, and strategies that help students feel safe in their classroom, believe in themselves as mathematicians, and think critically about their own and others' mathematical thinking. By implementing the structures and norms we suggest at the beginning of the year and reinforcing them throughout the year, you can help give your students a strong foundation upon which to build their mathematical understanding.

Chapter Two A Respectful Community of Learners

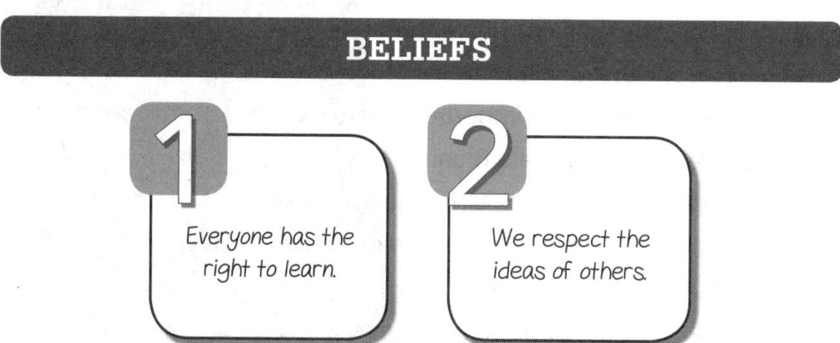

BELIEFS
1
Everyone has the right to learn.
2
We respect the ideas of others.

Classrooms that are truly rooted in student-centered learning are communities where students take control of their own learning by taking risks, thinking flexibly, and critiquing their own and others' ideas. In order for students to thrive successfully, the classroom culture must be one that fosters a deep level of respect from and for all learners.

Respect: Why It Matters

When a respectful atmosphere exists in the classroom, students feel more comfortable sharing their mathematical thinking with one another, taking risks, and tackling new ideas. All learners feel that they and their ideas are important.

The first step to building a respectful community of learners is to develop positive relationships between students as well as with the teacher. This can be accomplished in the beginning of the year through the careful use of relationship-building activities (see more below). Spending time getting to know your kids, their families, and their interests also helps form these valuable relationships. Showing interest in our students lets them know that we value them as individuals; it sets up an atmosphere in which students feel respected and cared for when they come to school.

Clear expectations are also essential in building a respectful community. These expectations should be created with the students. When students have a say in creating the expectations, they are more likely to internalize them. It requires time, effort, and lots of practice to set up and reinforce these expectations, but the time invested is more than made up for throughout the year. When expectations are clear and well established, you can focus more on increasing the depth of learning than on managing student misbehaviors.

Respect comes down to two core beliefs that both we and our students need to internalize: everyone has the right to learn, and we should all respect the ideas of others. In this chapter, we'll look at ways to build and reinforce both these beliefs.

Encouraging Respect Within the Classroom

In our classrooms, respect is the foundation by which we develop trust and a sense of safety both with our students and between our students. When we are all able to show respect for one another as learners, including the teacher, students feel safe and feel empowered to make decisions about their own learning. They feel free to take the kind of risks needed in order to deeply understand mathematical concepts.

Respect must be directly taught to students and needs to be reinforced throughout the year. We teach respect specifically through modeling and targeted praise. We show students that we respect them by providing them with opportunities to make their own decisions and honoring the decisions they make. In our classrooms, respect is at the heart of every interaction we have with students and is the undercurrent through which we manage our classrooms.

USING READ-ALOUDS

Although the term *respect* is familiar to most people, we can't assume that students know what it means to be respectful to teachers and classmates. Before introducing and teaching our specific classroom beliefs about respectful learning, it is important to ensure that all the students in your classroom understand what it means to be respectful. Read-alouds are a helpful tool for discussing ideas and concepts related to respect.

One book we often use is *Chrysanthemum*, by Kevin Henkes. This is a story about a young mouse who loves her unique name, Chrysanthemum. Her feelings change when she attends school and all her classmates begin to make fun of her long, unusual name. Throughout the story, Chrysanthemum shows us what it feels like to be on the receiving end of disrespectful treatment. Chrysanthemum's story is something students can relate to and provides an opportunity for us to discuss how important it is to respect differences in our classroom.

After reading this book aloud, we have students brainstorm ideas of respect and we chart them on a two-column poster, sorting the ideas into what respect looks like and what it sounds like. Adding students' names to their ideas on the poster helps them feel invested in their definitions of respect (see Figure 2.1). Having the students participate in creating classroom expectations allows for more accountability because students are thinking through *why* these expectations are important instead of just listening to a teacher *tell* them they are important. It also helps students feel that their ideas are important and respected.

Chrysanthemum isn't the only book that can be used to teach respect. A quick internet search will give you plenty of ideas for read-alouds that touch on concepts of respect. Some of our other favorites are *How Full Is Your Bucket?*, by Tom Rath and Mary Reckmeyer; *Miss Nelson Is Missing!*, by Harry Allard; *Hooway for Wodney Wat*, by Helen Lester; and *Yoko*, by Rosemary Wells.

Figure 2.1:
"Looks Like"/"Sounds Like" Chart

EVERYONE HAS THE RIGHT TO LEARN

Once students have a basic understanding of what respect means, we can move on to teaching more in-depth lessons about respect for others during math time. One of the most important concepts of respect within the math community is that every student has the right to learn. It is our job to help students understand that in a community of learners, we must be mindful of how other students learn and how our behavior may affect the learning of others.

At the beginning of the year in Mrs. Dance's fourth-grade class, she begins a discussion of respect by asking students to think about ways they help out their families at home.

> Mrs. Dance: *Okay, friends, we are so lucky to be here together in Room 7 because it's almost like we have another family here at school. We get to spend a lot of time together, which means we need to talk about how we will work together as a family. Let's start by thinking about the ways that you help out your families at home. Turn to your partner and have your "mustard" partner start by explaining how they help out their family members at home.* [Students have been identified as "mustard" or "ketchup" to specify who will partner with whom, and who will speak first in pair shares.]

The students explode with discussion while talking about this concrete idea.

> Mrs. Dance: *Okay, my "ketchup" kids: I hope you were listening to your partner because I want you to tell me one way that your partner helps their family at home.*
>
> Elijah: *David empties the dishwasher and then loads it after dinner.*
>
> Mrs. Dance: *That's an excellent way to help! Can you come to my house, David?*
>
> Anastasia: *Natalie helps her mom make tacos by shredding the cheese.*
>
> Mrs. Dance: *Families care for each other and help each other just like Natalie helps her mom make tacos. Our*

While the students share out their partner's ways of helping at home, Mrs. Dance charts the ideas and later posts the chart in the classroom. This chart can then be used by the teacher as an idea source for writing contextual math problems based on the students' real lives throughout the year.

main job in our classroom family is to learn and be the best classmates we can be. Every single one of us is very important in this family, and every one of us has both the right and the responsibility to learn. We have to help each other and be our best selves, so that everyone can learn as much as possible. It is our job to make sure that everyone is treated with respect, so they all can learn to their highest capacity. What do you think are some ways that we can help our classmates do their best? Ketchup partners, you share first, and mustard partners, you will share out their ideas.

After the turn and talk (see Figure 2.2), students share their suggestions with the class.

Colten: *Damian said we need to raise our hands instead of calling out the answer.*

Mrs. Dance: *Thanks, Colten. Why would it be important to raise our hands and not call out the answer?*

Colten: *Well, if we call out the answer, we aren't waiting our turn.*

Mrs. Dance: *You're right, we aren't waiting our turn and we're taking away someone else's chance to share. Anything else?*

Figure 2.2: Students Turning and Talking During Carpet Time

The students continue sharing ideas like helping a friend find a different spot if they are distracted at their table and staying quiet during tests. With each suggestion, Mrs. Dance helps students understand why these ideas help show respect to classmates. Again, these ideas are charted and the chart is added to throughout the year as new ideas emerge.

In order to reinforce these important ideas, we use a series of teaching moves and routines throughout the year that support all students' right to learn.

Private Think Time

We know that everyone processes information differently. Some students learn best by talking through ideas with a partner, but others need quiet, independent think time to process ideas. We also know that students won't even try to think about finding the answer to a question if they know their teacher will call on the first person that raises their hand.

It is important to give ample wait time, about eight to twelve seconds, to students after asking a question. This can be one of the hardest things to do as a teacher as we sit quietly, letting the silence hang in the air. When we ask a question and wait, we are giving everyone a chance to think through their answer and decide how they would like to respond. This is especially helpful for English learners and students who may take longer to process information. We tell our students that we all think and learn at different paces, so as teachers we need to give them the time they need to think.

Once you promise your students that you will respect their need to think and always provide them with the think time they deserve, they begin to expect it. Tell them that if you forget, they can remind you. One concrete way to have students help you remember to provide wait time is to have them positively reward you every time you give them the think time they need. Let them give you a tally mark on the board when you remember to give them their think time. This is not something you would do with every question as the tallies may become overwhelming, but for a short period of time it is a great way to both build community and increase your wait time.

It's also important to make clear to students that we expect them to use this think time for thinking! To hold all students accountable for thinking through a response during this private think time, we have our students give a thumbs-up on their tummy ("private thumb" or "secret silent signal") when they are ready with their response to a question. With a private signal, students aren't distracted by their neighbors waving their hands in the air and don't feel panicked that others have the answer when they are still thinking. We take the time to explain this expectation to our students, to help them understand that we are asking them to keep their signals silent and private to show respect for others' need to think.

Different visual signals can be used to show different levels of understanding as well. We might ask students to give a thumbs-down, meaning "I don't have the answer *yet*" (see Chapter 3 for more on this important addition!), or a sideways thumb, meaning "I have an answer, but I can't justify it yet," and so on.

We also make a point of giving all students private think time with a math problem before they begin work with a small group or a partner. We acknowledge that many students need to think through a problem before they begin partner work and ask that all students work quietly to respect the independent time these learners need. Again, it is important to explicitly tell your students why this independent think time is so essential. When they know why you are asking them to do something, they are more likely to follow through.

It is also important to stress taking our time with math tasks and assessments. We praise our learners for slowing down and thinking deeply with one problem rather than rushing through to get to the answer. If we hear a student call out, "I'm done!" we say, "When a mathematician thinks they're done, their work has just begun!" and encourage them to check their work, try another strategy, or justify their thinking more clearly. This idea is further discussed in Chapter 4.

"Don't Steal My Thinking!"

It is not uncommon for students to want to shout out an answer as soon as they have it. From day one, we explain that it is not respectful to call out an answer in class. In our classrooms, shouting out the answer is like "robbing" or "stealing" our classmates' chance to think and learn. We remind our students that everyone has the right to learn and calling out answers takes that right away from their classmates.

Equating shouting out an answer to stealing makes it very clear that this behavior is unacceptable. With time and reinforcement students begin to respect this idea. In fact, it is not uncommon for outbursts to occur when answers are shouted out. "You stole my chance to learn!" or "Don't take my thinking time away!" might be phrases you hear from your students. When this happens, we teach our students how to rephrase their disappointment with one another in a respectful way, such as "Please don't take away my chance to learn," or "Remember to raise your hand because I need thinking time, too."

We are not saying that our kids never call out (far from it!), but we constantly reinforce a quiet hand or a private silent signal to indicate when they have an answer ready. We positively reinforce these behaviors that give everyone the right to learn by simply acknowledging the action, praising it, or adding it to our two-column respect chart mentioned previously.

Turn and Talks

While we make an effort to provide quiet think time for our independent, introverted learners, we also need to provide our more extroverted learners with a chance to talk about their thinking as much as possible. The familiar "turn and talk" structure is one great way to build in time for this. Turn and talks also give students an opportunity to share their thinking in a smaller group before sharing it with the class. This is another scaffold for students who may not be ready or comfortable with sharing an idea with the whole class. It increases student voice in the room by providing an opportunity for more students to share ideas, instead of just one student answering a question for the whole class.

To facilitate successful turn and talks, allow students to choose one partner to be A and one B, or use creative alternatives like "peanut butter" and "jelly," or "ketchup" and "mustard." When starting a turn and talk, the labels can help the teacher be specific with how to structure the turn and talk conversation, identifying which partner should speak first and sometimes giving a signal for partners to switch listening and speaking roles. This can help keep one partner from dominating the conversation and helps make sure everyone has a chance to speak.

As the students participate in a turn and talk, we listen in to as many kids as we can. We ask questions to clarify or extend their thinking and look for students to share out common misconceptions or connections that we would like to have brought up in discussion. (For more on sharing student ideas, see Chapter 3; for more on questioning, see Chapter 5.)

Sometimes you may want to match students with similar levels of understanding. Other times, heterogeneous pairings are more useful. These partnerships help push the thinking of students who may be struggling with an idea, while those who have a good grasp of it are pushed to clarify their own thinking as they explain it to their partner. At still other times, you may let students choose their own partners, which can increase motivation and engagement. We also occasionally select short-term partnerships when we see that two students have used the same strategy but have a different answer, or when we see a disagreement and we would like the kids to justify their different solutions.

For long-term partnerships, we post a partner chart in the classroom so that students are aware of their partner and who to sit by on the carpet (see Figure 2.3). We attach the names with Velcro or sentence strips to allow us to make quick and easy changes to partnerships.

Turn and talk plays such an important role in our classrooms that we take a lot of time within the first few weeks of school to teach this routine. We begin by practicing with fun topics that allow us to get to know our students. Some examples include "What is your favorite ________? Why?" or "Would you rather ______ or ______? Why?" After a practice turn and talk, we ask the kids to reflect on what the turn and talk sounded like and looked like. We chart our "looks like" and "sounds like" ideas with the students' names. We then post this chart close to the carpet area (see Figure 2.4).

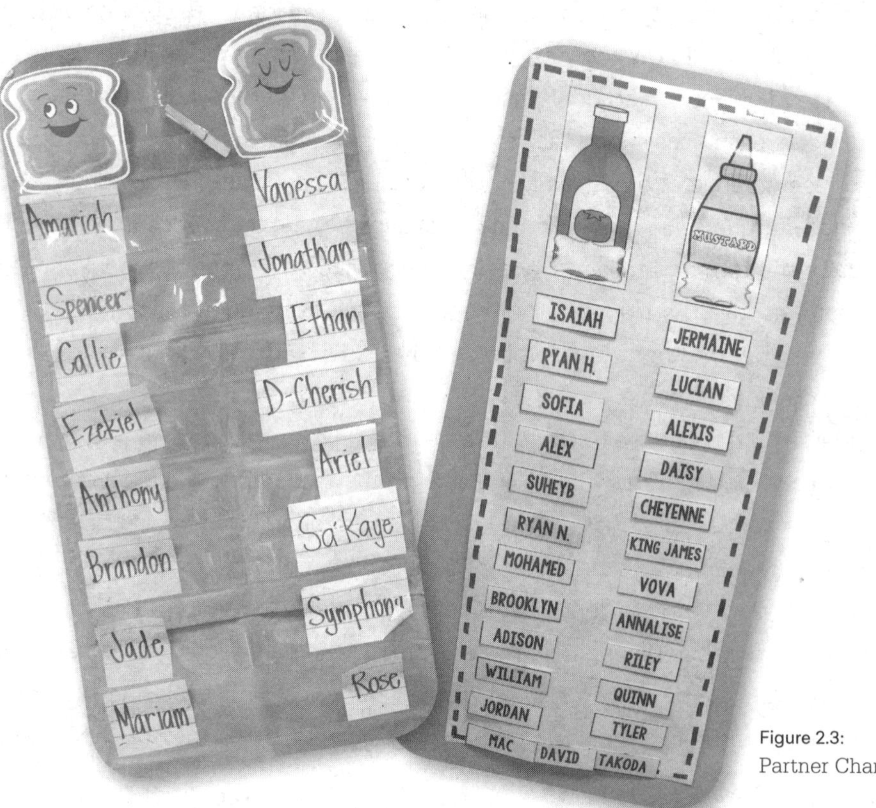

Figure 2.3:
Partner Charts

Figure 2.4: Turn and Talk Norms

> *It is important to set up a signal for getting the kids back to the whole group after a turn and talk. This may be a bell or some hand signal you use to get their attention. We like to use a hand signal that allows them to quickly finish up a sentence or thought before turning back to the whole group, instead of expecting them to abruptly stop talking midsentence. This demonstrates respect for their ideas and thoughts by allowing them a couple of seconds to wrap up their discussions.*

Once the expectations are listed and posted in the room, we continue to reinforce them by praising our learners when we see the behaviors in action. For example, we might say, "I love how Elijah and Mady are sitting face to face, knee to knee." You can add to the chart of expected behaviors throughout the year as kids come up with new expectations or you notice something that you would like to add.

How to Help a Partner

Because students work so often with partners and small groups, we also directly teach our students how to help one another without giving away an answer (because giving away the answer takes away the other student's chance to learn!). We work hard to help our students understand that they learn best when they figure out answers on their own. By reinforcing concepts of brain growth, including perseverance and struggle, we stress that we aren't learning if someone simply tells us the answer (more on this in Chapter 3). We make clear that we won't give them the answer, and we want them to be to able to trust that their classmates won't give them the answer when they ask for help, either.

We teach our students that when someone asks us for help, we must act as a math "coach," asking questions when someone is stuck or struggling instead of giving answers.

As a class, we brainstorm questions we could ask or things we could do to help our partner without "robbing" them of their thinking. We chart the students' suggestions and refer back to them often. We add to the chart throughout the year when we hear effective partner or group discussions.

Looks Like	Sounds Like
■ Both partners looking at the paper	■ "How did you get that as your answer?
■ Partners sitting side by side	■ "I respectfully disagree because ______."
■ Tracking the work with your finger or a pencil, so your partner can follow along	■ "Maybe you can count again to double-check."
■ Sharing the tools	■ "What other strategy could you use?"

We practice these routines repeatedly in the beginning of the year by having partnerships or groups work on a short task together and then bringing the whole class together to reflect briefly on how it went.

In Mrs. Dance's room, some fourth graders have just finished up a group task and are reflecting on what went well and what didn't.

> Mrs. Dance: *Turn to your partner and come up with one way you worked well together today and one thing you'd like to do better tomorrow.*
>
> The students refer to the partner work chart posted on the wall as they discuss how they worked together that day.
>
> Mrs. Dance: *Would anyone like to share with the group one thing you did well with your partner?*
>
> Sammy: *When I was feeling stuck, Marshal explained how he used an array to solve the problem. After he explained it, I understood and could solve the problem with a multiplication table.*
>
> Mrs. Dance: *Thanks, Sammy. Now, who would like to share a way that you'd like to work together better tomorrow?*

Lily: *When I was working with Mika, I didn't get to do any of the writing.*

Mrs. Dance: *Okay, what could Mika and Lily do tomorrow to make sure that both of them have a chance to write?*

Marcus: *They could make a plan. Decide who is going to draw the model and who is going to write the sentences.*

Mrs. Dance: *Great idea, Marcus. Mika and Lily, will that be a good goal for you tomorrow?*

Another way to reinforce positive partner behaviors is to acknowledge when students are productively working together. Occasionally, we stop the group and have students repeat their conversation while the class listens, or we ask if we can summarize their conversation and share it with the class after work time is over.

It also helps to have visuals posted of what good partner work looks like. You can take pictures of partners and groups helping each other (like the images in Figure 2.5) and post them with your "looks like" / "sounds like" chart. Discuss why these pictures exemplify good partner or group work so that students understand how to emulate the behavior.

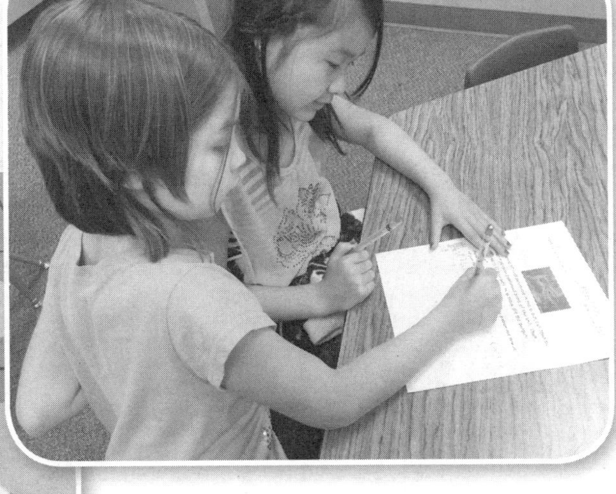

Figure 2.5:
Partnerships at Work

Revoicing/Retelling

Many important ideas and concepts are discussed during whole-group lessons, but many of our students have difficulty focusing during these whole-group times. It is our responsibility to acknowledge every student's right to learn by ensuring that they can access the information being discussed.

For students who have difficulty focusing, using revoicing or retelling as a talk move can help keep them engaged in the conversation. When an efficient strategy or an important big idea has been shared, we often have the kids turn to their partner and revoice the strategy or big idea in their own words. We then call on someone to repeat it to the class.

Rephrasing the idea for the whole class can help clarify student thinking and lets you see how well students understand their classmates' thinking. No matter how clear and concise a student's explanation may be (and we know they often are not!), we know that some students may be struggling to understand, so rephrasing allows another chance to hear and understand the ideas. This acknowledges everyone's right to hear and understand the important concept. It also promotes better student listening, since students are aware that you may call on them to repeat an idea. This is also something we do after a student has asked a valuable question. "Wow, that is a really good question. Did everyone hear what Trenton asked? Who can repeat Trenton's question, because someone else may have the same question?"

As mentioned previously, be explicit with your students about why you are asking them to repeat or rephrase another classmate's thinking. They need to understand that you are not trying to "catch them" not listening, but that you are trying to ensure that all students are understanding the concept at hand.

Honoring *All* Students' Thinking

We want our students to feel deeply that each and every individual in our classroom contributes in an important way to our mathematical community. Therefore, we honor all our students' thinking. We don't just look for the kid who always has the correct answer; instead, we look for different answers and different ways of solving a problem. We emphasize to students that we all learn and grow at different rates and in different ways. We model for our students how to respect the thinking of others, even when it seems confusing or wrong. For example, we might respond to a student sharing by saying, "Wow, I love how Julien drew circles yesterday to model the problem, but today he was brave and tried something new," or "I like how you showed your thinking with base ten blocks, but I'm having trouble understanding where the third hundred came from. Could you explain that more?" We also celebrate when students think differently from one another because it is through learning how others think that we increase our own mathematical knowledge. (We will return to this in Chapter 4.)

One thing we must constantly be aware of is who we are asking to share and how often. It may be challenging to find opportunities for some of our struggling learners to share, so we must get creative about finding ways to get their ideas in front of the class. For instance, if you have a student who rarely finishes his work, look for a time when this student makes good progress or has an interesting, even if partial, idea that you can have the child share. Celebrate that they made an attempt to solve the problem. For your students who tend to use the same strategy every day, ask them to share their strategy with the class, emphasizing how strongly the student understands that strategy. Then ask students to respectfully suggest other strategies that the child could try in order to stretch their brain a bit more. Always start by acknowledging the thinking that is in the work (there's always something!), then make suggestions for further growth.

Max Ray-Riek (2016) talks in a video posted to the Heinemann blog about a time in fifth grade when he was feeling apathetic and defeated about math in general. He spent a long time solving one problem and was feeling very frustrated, but his teacher asked him to share his thinking for that one problem. For Ray-Riek, that one experience opened his eyes to the world of math and helped him to believe in himself as a mathematician—and he now has published a book about problem-solving in math!

Also, be aware of your own (sometimes unrealized) biases as a teacher. How often are the boys sharing in your classroom versus the girls? Are you making sure that the students who represent a minority population in your classroom get a chance to share as often as others? Are you giving your students with IEPs a chance to share their thinking and providing them with the accommodations necessary to make that possible? You might consider keeping an ongoing list of who you ask to share each day. As you walk around the room looking for students to share their thinking with the whole class, keep your list handy. Make an effort to look for students to share who haven't shared in a while. It won't always work out perfectly, but making an effort shows your students that you respect them all as learners and find their mathematical thinking to be as valuable as everyone else's.

Revising Thinking

In our classrooms, as students share, we record their responses to show that we value everyone's thinking. These public records are posted throughout the room. However, we don't record just correct answers but misconceptions and incorrect solutions as well. When a misconception or incorrect solution is shared with the class, we work as a respectful community to help the child "revise" their thinking.

As students justify solutions or ask questions about others' thinking, they sometimes come to realizations about their own misconceptions. As a result of this, they want to change an incorrect answer. When this happens, we encourage students to say, "I'm revising my thinking" or "I need to revise my thinking." With practice and reinforcement, this language becomes common in the classroom. (We'll talk about this more in Chapter 3.)

By using this kind of language in the classroom, we show our students that we respect their right to make mistakes and change their thinking as they learn and grow. Instead of feeling defeated or upset when mistakes are made, they learn to take pride in their growth. When you begin to hear students exclaim, "I want to revise my thinking!" your teacher heart will melt every time.

RESPECT THE IDEAS OF OTHERS

When you open up your classroom to become an environment where mistakes and disagreements are celebrated, you run the risk of also opening students to unkind comments and shame from classmates. It is essential to teach your students that respecting the ideas of others means treating everyone with kindness and compassion, even when we disagree. As teachers we model respectful behavior with our tone of voice, our consideration for everyone, and most importantly our celebration of differences within our classroom. We seek out and celebrate times when our kids are helpful to one another. We praise students when they share thinking that is different from that of their classmates, and we love *respectful* disagreements.

Respectful Listening

Respectful listening is crucial within our mathematical community. We must model respectful listening in our classroom as well as teach it to our students. To teach respectful listening, we begin with a whole-group discussion about what it means to listen with your whole body. We explain that as a family we need to value each other, and one way we can do that is by really listening to what everyone says in class. We start with a chart that has a picture of a student sitting respectfully. While looking at the picture, we ask students to make observations about what they notice the respectful listener doing. Students often come up with ideas like "eyes on the speaker" and "ears listening."

We go on to talk about the importance of "still hands and bodies," explaining that often moving bodies distract not only the students doing the moving but also all the other students around them. We acknowledge that many students can listen and fidget at the same time, but we must respect how our fidgeting can distract our neighbors from learning. For students who need to move in order to learn, you could have them move to the back of the carpet area or to a chair that is still close enough to the sharing area but less distracting for others. Some students also work well with a stuffed animal or fidget toy after being taught how to hold it close so it doesn't distract others. With young students, you can remind them to "keep your cookies in your cookie jar" when using a fidget. This way, they know they can't throw it in the air or put it near other learners.

We encourage students to use the term "speaker" when talking about respectful listening instead of "teacher," because oftentimes the person doing the talking in our classrooms is not the teacher.

Beyond these physical, visible expectations, though, students often have trouble articulating what respectful listening is. We sometimes nudge the discussion by asking, "If we want to show our classmates respectful listening, what should our brain be doing?" This can be a new concept for some students. We share the example of a student sitting still and quiet with their eyes on the speaker, but they are thinking about what they want to play at recess. We acknowledge that just because we *look like* we are listening, it doesn't mean we always are listening.

We add one more important layer to our idea of listening with your whole body: in order to be a good listener, our hearts should be caring about what the speaker is saying, too. Not only do we respectfully listen, but we care about what our classmates have to say.

A great read-aloud to reinforce respectful listening is *Lacey Walker, Nonstop Talker*, by Christianne Jones. This is the story of a little owl who spends all her time talking until she loses her voice; it's during this time that she realizes all the cool things that happen when she actually listens rather than talks.

Respectful Disagreements

In our classrooms, we love and encourage disagreements in math. It is through these disagreements that students can grapple with tough mathematical concepts, explaining and justifying their ideas as they try to reach a resolution. We let our students know that disagreements are not a negative thing but something wonderful, as they show that we are thinking deeply about math, allowing our brains to grow stronger.

Looking at disagreements in a positive way allows you to set up a community of learners who are confident rather than anxious when their thinking is different than that of their neighbor or class, and who understand that a disagreement is different from a fight. However, not all students know how to disagree respectfully. When teaching students how to disagree, we encourage them to stay away from comments like "You're wrong," and encourage more positive comments like "I'm thinking differently." Having students model and role-play disagreements, with everyday ideas as well as mathematical concepts, can be a great way to teach respectful disagreement. Once students have practiced disagreeing and feel safe doing so, they become more adept at disagreeing with one another's ideas in a respectful way.

In Mrs. Dance's room, the fourth graders are having a disagreement about where $\frac{1}{2}$ fits on a number line that ranges from 1 to 2.

Danica: *I think it goes in the middle because $\frac{1}{2}$ is always in the middle.*

Mrs. Dance: *Can you silently show if you agree or disagree with Danica's thinking?*

Most of the class points to their foreheads, showing they are disagreeing, or thinking differently.

Mrs. Dance: *I'm seeing that a lot of students are thinking differently from Danica. Who would like to explain why? Eric?*

Eric: *Danica, I heard you say that you think $\frac{1}{2}$ goes in the middle, but I respectfully disagree. On this number line, 1 is in the middle because it goes all the way to 2.*

Danica: *What do you mean?*

Eric: *This number line starts at 0 and ends at 2, so the middle has to be 1, not $\frac{1}{2}$.*

Danica: [pausing and staring at the number line for a moment] *Oooooh, I need to revise my thinking. I thought the number line ended at 1.*

In this vignette, you can see that the students have practiced and internalized several phrases that help express respectful disagreement: "I heard you say . . . ," "I respectfully disagree . . . ," and "I need to revise my thinking" are all language that has been directly taught by Mrs. Dance. Danica also used a clarifying question when she was having difficulty following Eric's reasoning (see Chapter 5 for ideas on how to promote student questioning). As with other sentence stems, posting these near the whole-class discussion area enables students to refer to them, and therefore use them, often (more on sentence stems later in this chapter).

We also spend time discussing our tone of voice and how we can often convey feelings just by the way we say things. When we respond in an angry tone, people may react with anger in return. We practice using the disagreement stems both with a calm, kind tone of voice and with an angry tone of voice. Young students in particular love when the teacher models an angry tone of voice, because it seems so out of context to them. We talk about how differently the same phrase can be interpreted by the listener based on the tone of voice.

Once expectations about disagreements are in place, we seek out differences in thinking within our students' work. When we see students using different models or strategies to solve problems, we may say something like, "Your partner used a hundred chart to hop by tens, but you used a number line. Can they both be correct?" In this way, students are pressed to justify their thinking in order to resolve disagreements or identify differences/similarities between strategies (see Chapter 4 for ways to help students learn to justify thinking).

In Chapter 3, we will discuss some silent signals that can be used to express agreement and disagreement, along with ways to encourage mathematical disagreements.

Explaining Disagreements

Often, once students realize that disagreement is encouraged, they may begin to disagree simply to disagree (as young children often do). We teach our young mathematicians that we can't grow our brains by simply saying that we disagree. If we disagree, we must explain why. In fact, it can come across as disrespectful to classmates if students simply say "I disagree." Students who are sharing may feel their thinking is underappreciated if students are jumping to disagree with it without explaining why. By justifying our disagreements, we show respect, because we acknowledge others' thinking and then explain how ours differs. Sentence starters such as "I disagree with your thinking because . . ." or "I'm thinking differently because . . ." help students to frame their disagreements in respectful ways. It's also crucial to make sure that our students understand that we are disagreeing not with our classmates but just with their thinking.

Honoring Mistakes

Along with disagreements, we celebrate mistakes in our classrooms because it is through these misconceptions that children learn and make sense of new mathematical concepts. Because of this, we often have students share mistakes with the whole group. In order to set up a community where all students feel respected, we discuss appropriate and inappropriate ways to react to a classmate's mistake. Laughing at someone else's mistake is unacceptable, and if it happens, we address it firmly and directly. We thank children who make and share mistakes for the learning opportunity they have created for the class. In the next chapter, we will explain in detail the structures we put in place for celebrating and thinking through mistakes.

REINFORCING RESPECT

In order to maintain a respectful community, respectful behaviors must be reinforced consistently through modeling, praise, and explicit instructional strategies.

Modeling

Once you have decided on your expectations as a class, it is important to continually model these expectations yourself. If students are expected to keep a certain voice level, it is important that you as the teacher do the same. If the students decide that respect means eyes and ears on the speaker, the teacher should directly model this behavior as students are speaking and sharing. This also shows that as teachers we really care about what students have to say and are interested in their ideas.

There are likely to be times throughout the year, such as just before or after long breaks, when student behavior difficulties tend to increase. It is important during these times to reteach your classroom expectations through modeling. Students can model both non-examples and positive examples of an expected behavior. It is more valuable and there is more buy-in from the class when students practice modeling the ideas that they came up with.

Praise

Another way to reinforce respectful behavior is through direct, specific praise. No matter their age, kids of all grade levels always love positive praise! When we teachers praise students, we get to use our best enthusiastic acting skills. When you see a student using whole-body listening, respectfully disagreeing, or appreciating someone else's mistakes, praise that student in front of the whole group. This praise should be specific, naming the behavior and expressing why it is important. If we hear students using a respectful phrase, we might write it down and begin a public record of those phrases. Small and random incentives, such as stickers, tickets, or simply applause can also be given to reinforce a targeted behavior. We tend to go heavy on commending positive behaviors in the beginning of the year and then these behaviors become more innate with the students.

If you notice that students are starting to overlook certain expectations, begin your day or week by setting a behavior goal. Look for students throughout the day who are following the goal expectation and provide small incentives or praise.

Many teachers use some type of point system within the classroom to reward positive behavior. We assign table groups to be teams. Whenever we see someone on a particular team showing an expected behavior, we praise that student and then give the whole team points using a publicly posted tally chart system. For example, we might say, "I just heard Elijah on the green team say he respectfully disagrees with another teammate. Elijah, can you give your team 50 respect points, please?"

By awarding team points, students are encouraged to work together as a community. Students spend time reinforcing and reminding each other of the expectations in hopes of earning points as a team. We never provide rewards for the team that earns the most points, yet we have found that the simple accumulation of points and the praise involved in giving out points is enough to motivate classmates to work respectfully with each other. We also never take points away from a team. Once students have shown respectful behavior and earned those points, it is not fair for us as teachers to take those points away.

Public Records / Anchor Charts

As we mentioned earlier in this chapter, when we teach and reinforce expectations about respect within the classroom community, we often make anchor charts or public records of the students' thoughts, words, and ideas. We always make sure to record the name of the student who came up with a suggested behavior, to let them know we respect their input. It is also important that these charts are displayed prominently in the classroom and referred to regularly. When students fail to follow a certain expectation, we can remind them of our classroom expectations by pointing to the chart on the wall. This reminds them that we created these expectations as a class and we agreed to follow them. We also might add ideas to a chart throughout the year as new issues or problems arise. These public records of our ideas become a living, growing part of our classrooms. Students also help each other by referring to these charts and records after we've modeled their use.

Sentence Stems

Providing students with sentence stems is a great way to encourage respectful disagreements and promote everyone's right to learn. Often, students have not been taught how to respectfully engage with children of their own age. They may not have enough knowledge of language to successfully interact with their classmates. Providing sentence stems helps students learn to speak in respectful ways.

These stems may include

"I respectfully disagree because _____________."

"I solved the problem differently because ____________."

"I like how you __________ because ____________."

"I'm having trouble understanding how you ___________. Could you explain it in a different way?"

These sentence stems work best when they come from the students themselves. If a student speaks respectfully or asks a respectful question in math, we write it on a sentence strip and place it where it is accessible to all our learners during our math discussions. Make sure to give the student credit by adding their name to the sentence stem. However, students may not always be able to come up with these structures themselves, so there may be times where we provide them.

Encouraging Students to Reinforce Respect

Our goal as teachers is to help our students learn how to treat one another respectfully without needing our intervention as teachers. As mentioned before, we purposefully praise students who show respect, but we also specifically praise students who reinforce respect with one another. When they hear another student acting disrespectfully, we want our students to correct one another in a kind way.

When teaching respectful behavior expectations, we often develop silent classroom signals that represent certain behaviors, such as raising a hand or making a zero with our fingers to show a silent voice is expected. We teach these silent reminders to our students and encourage them to use them with each other. For instance, if a student's neighbor is talking during carpet time as someone is sharing, we encourage students to turn to one another and show a silent signal reminder instead of directly asking the student to stop talking. This helps students remember that they can work to keep a respectful environment in the classroom.

As teachers, we've all had that frustrated moment in front of the class when we simply stop and say, "I'm going to wait." Often in this circumstance students begin yelling at one another to quiet down. Voices may begin to escalate as we "wait" for attention. However, this strategy of waiting for the class to be ready can be helpful if students have been taught how to respectfully correct one another's behaviors. Once we have taught our students to give silent reminders to a student who is not paying attention, this teacher wait time can be extremely effective in encouraging students to reinforce respectful behaviors with one another. We might slowly and quietly begin thanking students who are giving those silent reminders until the class is showing the expected behaviors.

Once you tell the class that you will wait, you might set a quiet timer and time how long it takes for students to help one another show they are ready to learn. Set a time goal with your students and celebrate when they are able to quiet down more quickly. With time they will get better and better at reinforcing respectful behavior with one another.

We also encourage our students to monitor their classmates' behavior as they are sharing. Before a student begins to share their math thinking for the day, we ask that student to "check for respect." The student scans the group sitting on the carpet, giving respect reminders to students who need them. "Elisa, could you please cross your legs?" "Brianne, level-zero voice, please." We train students to begin sharing their thoughts only when they feel they have the full respect of the class. When students are able to do this, not only does it help reinforce the expectations, but it helps students understand what it looks like and sounds like when the whole class is ready to listen respectfully.

We might also ask students to do a "body check" as they are sitting on the carpet if we notice they are losing attention. When we stop a lesson or share and say "let's check our bodies," students will quickly fix their bodies to show whole-body listening. This helps students to self-monitor their own behavior.

When Things Don't Seem to Be Working

What do I do when a student keeps saying "You're wrong!"?

If we hear a student say something disrespectful such as "You're wrong," we ask them if they can rephrase it in a more respectful way. Directing students to the sentence stems posted in the room is a great resource for rephrasing disagreements respectfully. If a student persists with this kind of disrespectful talk, we will have a one-on-one conversation with them about how their comments affect their classmates. We might ask them to apologize and spend some time reflecting on what they might say next time instead.

What do I do when students have trouble retelling or repeating thinking?

When students struggle to rephrase their classmates' thinking, encourage them to think of a question they can ask to help clarify what the student sharing is trying to say. Ask, "What questions can we ask _______ to better understand [his/her] thinking?"

You may also want the first student to share again, or you may want to provide more time for your students if you notice that they are not able to repeat. Another option is to call on a different student to rephrase thinking, encouraging the student who is struggling to listen carefully to another student's rephrasing. You can then then ask the initial student to try again to rephrase something in their own words. Practicing retelling/rephrasing with other topics of discussion also helps the kids become more familiar with this routine.

It can also help to remind students that you will be asking them to retell their classmate's thinking before the student shares. You might say, "Remember, after Sasha is done sharing, I am going to ask you to turn to your partner and tell them how Sasha solved the problem." This can help students focus and think more deeply about their classmate's strategy as it is being shared.

What do I do when one student keeps taking over during turn and talks?

When this happens, you may need to have a conversation with this partner pair, giving them strategies to use to help them remember to take turns. You might suggest that the more talkative partner always talk second even if the teacher assigns a different partner to talk first. You might also keep this group seated close to you on the carpet so that you can give quick reminders during turn and talk times that one student needs to wrap up so that the other one has time to talk.

Giving each partner a specific and equal amount of time to talk can also help prevent one student from taking over. Turn and talks are very important in our math discussions and require a lot of modeling. Praising those partnerships that are equitable with talking and listening tends to encourage others to do the same.

What do I do when students call out the answer to a question?

Especially at the beginning of the year, we have a lot of thinking "thieves" who call out the answer before some students have even read the problem. When this happens, we calmly remind these students of our expectations and why they are important. This behavior often decreases as we continue to build community and place emphasis on everyone's right to learn, but once in a while there is a student who gets so excited they can't help themselves. Often, the students begin to reinforce this expectation among themselves, and more often than not our students who tend to call out the answer are conquered by peer pressure.

What do I do when a student laughs at someone's mistake?

If there is a respectful community created in your classroom that celebrates mistakes, this doesn't happen often, but if you find a student laughing at a mistake, you might invite them to leave the math community and then talk to them personally about how they would feel if someone treated them this way. With behavior like this, we are often firm and direct with students. We explain that laughing at someone's mistakes is not acceptable in our classroom and that there will be consequences if the behavior continues. It is crucial that the class understands that mistakes are a wonderful thing that we want shared in order for us to grow our brains. (We give some more tips on this in Chapter 3.)

Summary

Cultivating a classroom community where students treat each other and the teacher with respect and compassion is essential to the development of a problem-solving-based mathematical community. Students must understand what it truly means to show respect to one another. They must understand that every student in our classroom has a right to learn, and that sometimes our choices and our actions can take away that right. As teachers, we must directly teach and reinforce respectful behavior throughout the year. Once your classroom has developed into a respectful community of learners, students will feel the intellectual safety they need to start thinking deeply about mathematics.

Chapter Three **Building Brave Mathematicians**

BELIEFS
3
Challenging problems help our brains grow stronger.
4
Mistakes are great!
5
Good mathematicians are brave and try new things.

Picture three students as they tackle a challenging math problem. Yolanda finishes quickly with little struggle. Irma tackles the problem several times before finally figuring it out and smiling with pride. Sabrina gets frustrated on the first try, feeling as though she isn't smart enough to solve the problem. She eventually copies a neighbor, so she can get an answer on her paper.

As you picture these three girls, who would you say learned the most from the problem? Sabrina gave up immediately and just copied an answer. Yolanda finished quickly and got the answer right, but did she learn anything new? What might happen if she was confronted with a problem she didn't know how to solve—would she persevere or give up when confronted with the new challenge? It's hard to tell. Now think about Irma, who struggled and persevered until she finally solved the problem. She made a few mistakes along the way but was not discouraged by them and continued working until she figured it out. When we teach math to young children, it is our job to create a classroom community where all our students have mathematical confidence and perseverance.

Mathematical Confidence: Why It Matters

In order for children to make sense of math, they must believe that they are capable of understanding and learning math. There is a pervasive belief in our culture that being good at math is an innate ability. However, researchers like Carol Dweck have worked hard to disprove this belief. According to Dweck (2006), people with a fixed mindset believe that our abilities and intelligence cannot be changed, while people with a growth mindset believe that our abilities can be changed through study, practice, and hard work. As teachers, we need to reinforce a growth mindset in our students. Mathematical confidence reflects a growth mindset and includes a willingness to persevere, a positive attitude toward mistakes, a willingness to take risks, and self-reliance.

PERSEVERANCE

Children's mathematical confidence affects their approach to challenges and failure. Children with low self-confidence may fail or make a mistake and define themselves by that failure, deciding that they are not smart. When faced with a challenge, these children may get angry and give up because they feel they are not smart enough to figure it out. On the contrary, students who see themselves as "smart" may believe that any struggle means that they are not smart. This may lead them to seek to preserve their sense of "smartness" by avoiding something that might take work.

Children who possess mathematical confidence look at challenging math problems in a completely different way. Failure is a chance to learn and grow. It is a chance to reflect and think, "What can I do better next time?" Common Core Mathematical Practice Standard 1 asks children to "make sense of math problems and persevere in solving them" (CCSSO 2010). Children with mathematical confidence are able to persevere through challenging problems, trying and trying again until they figure them out. It is our job as teachers to help them gain this perseverance.

VALUING MISTAKES

Fear of making mistakes, and being labeled as "wrong" or "failing," is one of the greatest obstacles to perseverance and to mathematical confidence. When students fear mistakes, it halts their ability to truly problem-solve. They are hesitant to try a strategy because they don't know for sure that it will get them the right answer. Children who have strong math confidence are unafraid to make mistakes. They know that mistakes are stepping-stones that help us learn. Jo Boaler, in her book *Mathematical Mindsets*, discusses brain research that shows how our brain grows and develops each time we make a mistake. When students solve a problem and get the answer right, no new neural pathways are formed. However, when a student makes a mistake, synapses in the brain fire, forming new pathways and connections. Most surprisingly, new brain pathways are formed from making mistakes *even when we don't know we are making them* (Boaler 2016). Boaler's research shows us that children and adults learn most when they are challenged and make mistakes. In a math classroom, mistakes should be celebrated as "great mistakes!" and learning opportunities, not looked at as simply wrong answers.

TAKING RISKS

To be successful mathematicians, young children also need to learn to be brave with new ideas. They need to feel confident enough to take risks, try new strategies, and share their thinking even when it contradicts that of others. When students believe in themselves enough to take mathematical risks, they know that if one strategy doesn't work, they can always try another. They feel confident that if they don't get it right the first time, they'll be able to figure out a way to solve the problem eventually. When a new, unfamiliar strategy is suggested, they are willing to give it a go. Helping students develop the confidence they need in math will allow them to take the risks necessary to truly make sense of mathematics.

SELF-RELIANCE

When students feel brave as mathematicians, they do not rely on the teacher to tell them what to do or how to solve a problem. They do not look for confirmation of their answers but instead check their own work and justify their thinking. We need to help them develop the mathematical confidence to persevere through tough problems, embrace productive mistakes, and challenge themselves by trying new strategies and ideas without constantly looking to the teacher for the answers.

Encouraging Mathematical Confidence

It is our responsibility as teachers to help set up a classroom environment that allows students to feel confident in their mathematical abilities as they persevere, make mistakes, and take risks with new ideas. When students possess this confidence, little stands in the way of their mathematical development. Below are some ways to begin building this environment for your students.

EVALUATING AND DISCUSSING SELF-CONFIDENCE

At the beginning of the school year, one of the most important things we do as teachers is get to know our children. It is during this "get to know you" time that we can easily learn about our students' confidence levels. You can learn how your students perceive themselves as mathematicians through discussions or a short survey. A math attitude survey could include a rating scale that students use to agree or disagree with statements such as "I enjoy math" or "math is useful" (see Figure 3.1 and Appendix A). It is best to give students the opportunity to independently fill out these surveys on paper so that they feel safe to be honest. For primary students, images like emojis or smiley faces can be used to help them think about their ratings.

Once you have gauged your students' confidence levels, introduce the idea that everyone can learn math, even if they feel like they aren't good at it.

Begin by encouraging students to think about something they are good at doing now that they weren't always good at. Examples they often come up with are playing a particular sport, riding a bike, or reading. Then encourage students to think about all the things they had to do to get better at that particular activity. To ride a bike, they probably had to have an adult's support as they learned to balance. Then they needed to practice in order to get better and better at staying up on their own.

Math Attitude Survey			
When I don't know what to do in math, I keep trying.	Yes	Sometimes	No
I share my thinking with others in math.	Yes	Sometimes	No
Math can be done in different ways.	Yes	Sometimes	No
I use math only at school.	Yes	Sometimes	No
I like math.	Yes	Sometimes	No
I can be good at math.	Yes	Sometimes	No
I talk to others in class about my ideas to solve math problems.	Yes	Sometimes	No

Figure 3.1: Math Attitude Survey

This activity can then be extended by having students think about things they are "good at" and things they are "not good at." Encourage them to make a list and think deeply about their strengths and some of the areas they struggle with. Finally, ask them where "doing math" would fall in their two categories. Some may indicate that they feel confident in math, but many will say that they are not good at it.

Close the discussion by relating math to the initial activity they thought about. Math is just like learning how to ride a bike. Students may feel like they are not good at it right now, but with practice and perseverance they will learn and grow as mathematicians.

READ-ALOUDS AND VIDEOS

We've found one of the best ways to teach students about self-confidence and perseverance is through good-quality read-alouds. By reading and discussing books with your class that address concepts of growth mindset, confidence, and perseverance, you can help students relate these ideas to how they think about math. Referring back to these read-alouds throughout the year can also be helpful reminders as kids struggle with their math confidence. Some of our favorite books to read at the beginning of the year are listed below.

- *Your Fantastic Elastic Brain,* by JoAnn Deak. In this book, Deak begins by introducing the brain as the organ that controls what we think, feel, and do. She talks about how we can create new pathways and connections in our brains to make them grow stronger and addresses making mistakes, learning through practice, and other important growth-mindset messages.
- *Koala Lou,* by Mem Fox. In this story, Koala Lou tries her hardest to win the Bush Olympics and impress her mom. In the end, she doesn't win but learns that her mom is proud of her hard work anyway. This is a great book on perseverance and making mistakes.
- *Leo the Late Bloomer,* by Robert Kraus. Leo is a lion who isn't very good at doing much of anything. His father is worried, but his mother knows that Leo will be able to do all these things when he is ready. This book helps children understand that we all learn at different paces.

- ***The Little Engine That Could,*** by Watty Piper. We all know the story of the little engine that could. No one believes that the little engine will be able to pull the long train over the mountain, but he believes in himself and is able to do it.

Videos are also another great resource for teaching and encouraging confidence in children. Jo Boaler's website (www.youcubed.org) has many videos that introduce the idea of growth mindset and relate it to math. ClassDojo (https://ideas.classdojo.com) has a series of animated videos on growth mindset and perseverance. Trevor Ragan also created a website (http://trainugly.com/growth-mindset-hub) geared toward older children with videos and resources for encouraging growth mindset and perseverance.

PERSEVERANCE IN THE REAL WORLD

Students do not often see perseverance in movies, TV shows, and the general media. They often will see the final success stories of characters or famous celebrities, but they don't hear of the hard work and failures that went into those successes. It is important for students to understand that very few people achieve fame or success the first time they try. Students need to be exposed to the stories of people who failed and persevered in order to succeed.

One way to help is to have students brainstorm a list of their favorite celebrities, inventors, and heroes. Once you have a list, do some class research on one or two of the people on their lists. Often, when researching these famous people, you will be able to find stories of hard work and perseverance. Sometimes students will choose someone who may have easily succeeded, and in this case you may discuss why that particular person found success so easily. It's true that sometimes people just get lucky, but it's important to discuss that this doesn't happen often and we can't rely on luck to succeed. You might have students think about what aspects of a person's life enabled their success or paved the path for them.

Again, literature has many great resources that tell the stories of famous people who struggled. One great book is *Snowflake Bentley*, by Jacqueline Briggs Martin, which tells the story of Wilson Bentley, who was the first photographer to successfully take a picture of a snowflake. Other famous figures who struggled at first include Albert Einstein,

Thomas Edison, Oprah Winfrey, and J. K Rowling, who submitted *Harry Potter and the Philosopher's Stone* to twelve publishing houses before one finally agreed to publish it. When we point out to children that some of the most successful people they know of had to work hard and persevere in order to achieve their goals, they begin to understand the value of their own hard work and mistakes.

Articles about some of the most successful tech companies have described how they encourage their employees to make mistakes and admit to them. Encourage your intermediate students to research how some companies are beginning to reward and celebrate the mistakes of their employees.

You can also promote perseverance by bringing up your own experiences with mistakes and struggles. Students always love to hear your stories and experiences, and they leave a lasting impression. It can be incredibly powerful for students to hear how their own teacher has struggled through tough times and challenges!

LANGUAGE USE

As teachers, we must pay close attention to the language we use with our students. When we are trying to help students develop confidence as learning and growing mathematicians, we are very careful to praise students not for their intelligence but for their perseverance and effort. When we praise students for their intelligence, saying things like "You're so smart" when they get a correct answer, students begin to identify themselves as "smart" or "not smart." When the smart students can't figure out an answer, they begin to believe that they are no longer smart. They face failure with the idea that they are not smart, instead of thinking they need to persevere through the difficulties until they succeed.

Carol Dweck says in her article "The Perils and Promises of Praise," "Research shows that that educators cannot hand students confidence on a silver platter by praising their intelligence. Instead, we can help them gain the tools they need to maintain their confidence in learning by keeping them focused on the *process* of achievement" (2007, 39). In our classrooms, we can focus our praise on hard work, perseverance, risk-taking, and questioning. Instead of praising students for getting the right answer, we praise them for being brave with a new strategy and working hard to solve the problem.

Student Language

The language students use among themselves must be addressed as well. When students are developing their skills as confident mathematicians, we must help them develop their mindset for math by shaping their language.

One common phrase that we hear students use is "I can't . . ." This simple phrase says so much about the way students perceive their abilities and skills. As Carol Dweck pointed out in a TED Talk, there's a simple way to change this by adding one word: when a student says, "I can't . . . ," we say, ". . . yet" (2014). The power of the word *yet* has an almost immediate effect on children's perceptions of themselves. In our early years of teaching, we outlawed the words "I can't . . ." in our classrooms, thinking that if children couldn't say it, they wouldn't believe it. This strategy however, failed to acknowledge children's current struggles with a task—telling them that they *can* do something they feel they *can't* doesn't provide them with a path toward success. When we began allowing "I can't . . ." and instead added ". . . yet" to the end of these utterances, we saw students' confidence levels begin to change. Instead of seeing success as a two-trail path where you get it or you don't, students began to see the path to success as a bumpy, windy, hilly trail that at times may seem impassable. The word *yet* allows students to push themselves through the seemingly impassable parts of the trail until they come out on the other end thinking, "I can!"

There is one other phrase that we pay close attention to, especially at the beginning of the year. Often, when confronted with a problem they understand right away, students will excitedly exclaim, "This is easy!" This phrase is problematic for two reasons. First, a problem that is easy for one student most likely is not easy for all students in the classroom. The child who struggles with a particular problem and hears a classmate exclaim, "This is easy!" immediately feels less confident about their own skills and abilities. Second, this phrase is troublesome because if the problem is easy, the student isn't learning!

We approach tackling "this is easy" language in two different ways to deal with both issues regarding the phrase. First, when a student says, "This is easy," our initial response is "Oh, no!" With surprised and apologetic looks on our faces, we say, "I'm sorry I didn't challenge your brain enough today. I'll have to find a problem for you that isn't so easy!"

We take the blame, emphasizing that when the problem is easy, students aren't learning anything new. We give the impression to our students that we don't want to waste their valuable learning time by asking them to solve problems they already know how to do. Students begin to understand that math problems *shouldn't* be easy at school, and when they are, the teacher needs to provide more difficult problems.

Additionally, it is important to discuss with the whole class at the beginning of the year how their exclamations of "This is easy!" affect their classmates. The first time this phrase comes up, we address it clearly and directly right away. We remind our students that we all learn at different paces and in different ways, and just because a problem may be easy for one student doesn't mean it's easy for all. We ask students to think about how a student who doesn't find the problem easy might feel when their friends say it is. To make this more concrete for younger learners, find a problem that is way too hard for the class as a whole. With gusto, act out reading the problem and exclaiming "This is so easy!" Have students discuss with each other what feelings bubble to the surface as they hear someone else say a problem they find extremely difficult is easy. By placing themselves in their classmates' shoes, they can begin to empathize with them. This helps set up a community of kindness and promotes respect for our different paces of learning. (For more on building respect in your classroom, see Chapter 2.)

Sharing your personal experience as a teacher can also help students understand the harmful effect of their words. Mrs. Dance tells her class about a time in PE when she struggled with the crab walk, which her classmates felt was easy. She shares her embarrassment and the students empathize with her, referring to the story often when a classmate tries to say, "This is easy."

Encouraging Perseverance

Let's take a look into Ms. Kaplan's classroom as some of her students are persevering through a difficult problem. She is listening in as a group of students begins working on the following problem: "Ms. Kaplan is trying to figure out if she has enough snacks to last the rest of the week. She has 3 bags of pretzels. Each bag has 100 pretzels. How many pretzels does she have?"

> Bohdan: *I think we should draw a picture of all the pretzels and count them.*
>
> Yosef: *I don't think so, that's going to take a really long time.*

Bohdan: *Then what should we do?*

Yosef: *I don't know . . . can we use a tool?*

Bohdan: *Connecting cubes?*

Yosef: *Okay.* [He jumps up a grabs a bin of cubes.]

Ms. Kaplan walks away, planning to come back and check in with the boys after they've worked a bit with the cubes. When she returns 5 minutes later, the boys have counted out about 150 cubes, but are running out of both cubes and table space. She decides to step in.

Ms. Kaplan: *Can you tell me about what you're doing to solve the problem?*

Yosef: *Well, Bohdan wanted to draw pictures of all of the pretzels in the bags, but I knew that wasn't a very efficient strategy for such a big number, so we decided to get connecting cubes.*

Bohdan: *Now we're counting out 100 connecting cubes for each bag, but I don't think it's going to work.*

Ms. Kaplan: *Why not?*

Bohdan: *There's not enough cubes and it's taking a long time.*

Ms. Kaplan: *So you need an even more efficient strategy?*

Bohdan: *I think so . . .*

Ms. Kaplan *Are there any other tools you could use that might be more efficient?*

The boys pause for a moment, looking toward the math center.

Yosef: *Base ten blocks?*

Ms. Kaplan: *How would those be more efficient?*

Yosef: *We could count by tens instead of ones. That would be faster.*

Ms. Kaplan: *Okay, why don't you give that a try and see how it goes.*

A few minutes later, the boys have made several groups with 10 ten rods in each group. Ms. Kaplan comes back to check on them again.

> **Ms. Kaplan:** *How are the base ten blocks working out?*
>
> **Bohdan:** *I think it's faster.*
>
> **Yosef:** *And look! Each group has 100, so you can skip count! 100, 200, 300 . . .*
>
> **Ms. Kaplan:** *Wow, it's great how you both persevered and tried out a few strategies before you found one that worked. Can you share with the class today and tell them how you wanted to draw pictures, then tried cubes, and then used base ten blocks?*

Notice how Ms. Kaplan allows the boys to struggle and seek out the correct tools on their own. They work their way through three strategies before finding one that works. When they finally are able to work through the problem, Ms. Kaplan praises them for their perseverance, not for their correct answer. Then she asks them to share their thinking with the class, specifying that she'd like them to share how they persevered with multiple strategies, not just sharing the one strategy that finally worked. In doing this, Ms. Kaplan puts the perseverance at the forefront of the whole-class conversation. This type of sharing and reinforcement can be done throughout the year.

CELEBRATING MISTAKES

One way to encourage students to embrace mistakes and learn from them is to ask students who have made common mistakes to share their thinking with the class. In the first week or two of school, as students are working on a difficult problem, look for a student who is fairly confident already to share a mistake they've made on a math problem. (For example, maybe the student drew 7 circles instead of 8 because they forgot to check their drawing.) Ideally, it should be a mistake that you see several students making, so that more of the class will relate to the student who shares. It is important that the first student to share a mistake for the year be one who already shows signs of confidence in math and is okay with sharing that they made a mistake. Be sure to talk with the student prior to sharing and privately discuss the importance of sharing mistakes with others so that the student is prepared to discuss the mistake in front of the class. While you will later choose all students to share mistakes, sharing a mistake for the first time can be daunting, since most students will not come in with the idea that mistakes are great!

Before the student shares, prep your class with a whole-group discussion about mistakes. Remind them that mistakes help our brains grow and that when we make a mistake we just make our brains stronger. Then tell the class that you have a student who has decided to be very brave and share a mistake they made while persevering through a problem. Emphasize how proud you are of this student for being so brave. Thank the student profusely in front of the class for sharing. You can't overdo the praise here in this first difficult share.

After the student shares, thank them again by saying, "Wow! That was such a great mistake!" Turn to the class and ask the students how many other students made that same mistake. Encourage students to be brave and raise their hands. This both reassures the student who is sharing and opens the gates for the rest of the class to begin owning the fact that we all make mistakes. Again, you can't overdo the praise here. Say things like, "Thank you so much for helping us all learn from your great mistake today!" Label your public record of student strategies with the words "Great mistake!" for this student. Have the class cheer and snap for the student for being so brave. You will not have to make such a big deal in the future for students who share mistakes, but for the first few times you need to ensure that the students understand how important it is to be brave, share your mistakes, and help others learn from them.

Pointing out our own mistakes when we make them as teachers can also be powerful. We often follow our mistake with, "I'm so glad I did that because I just learned something and I know I probably won't make that mistake tomorrow."

Continue to call mistakes "great mistakes" throughout the school year. You will notice your students begin to use this term with one another. "I notice that you made a great mistake here!" and "Thanks for sharing that great mistake!" will be phrases that you begin to hear around the classroom if you continue to reinforce this norm throughout the school year. As students become more comfortable making mistakes, be sure to reinforce the idea that while making the mistake is valuable, the most important idea is to reflect upon it and learn from it.

Finding Mistakes

Once students are comfortable with the idea that mistakes are great, it is important that they begin to notice them on their own. As with self-correcting while reading, we want our students to notice when they are making a mistake and make attempts to remedy it. One way to get students to begin looking for mistakes is to have them "find the mistake" that a classmate made in their work. When students are problem-solving during a work session, look for a student who is showing a common misconception in their work. Ask this student to share. Before they share, tell the students that the child who is sharing has made a mistake in their work. Their job is to be detectives and see if they can figure out the mistake that was made. Have them search for the common misconception instead of simply telling them.

Another option is sharing student work from a student you had previously in a different class. Share with your class that this was work from a previous student who has given you permission to share their "great mistake" with this year's class. Then you can go through the same routine of looking for and talking about the mistake. This works well if the students in your class seem especially sensitive to making mistakes or if your class is still learning to embrace their own mistakes.

After you have practiced finding mistakes a few times, you will begin to notice that your students will look for "great mistakes" in their classmates' work. Be sure you continually compliment any child who makes or shares a great mistake, and be conscious of keeping the attitude toward making and correcting mistakes very positive.

Thinking Through a Mistake

You can take finding mistakes a step further by asking students to think through the cause of a mistake. Practice thinking through a mistake by giving students an incorrect answer to a problem. Their task is to figure out what the student could have done in order to produce the incorrect answer. This process does several things for your students. First, it acknowledges that mistakes can come from good thinking. Just because a mistake was made doesn't mean that deep mathematical thought didn't go into it. Second, thinking through a problem in order to figure out the root cause of someone else's mistake demonstrates and develops deep mathematical understanding of the concept.

RESPECTFUL DISAGREEMENT

Inevitably, as students begin sharing and pointing out mistakes, disagreements will arise. The first time this happens, step in and teach students about the value of mathematical arguments. We always tell our students that we *love* arguments during math time. When they look at us in shock for saying this, we remind them that we all think differently and that by arguing we are learning to understand how other people think. We tell students that when they disagree with one another, they are being brave and standing up for their own thinking. And if it turns out that their thinking was a great mistake, we all get to learn from both the argument *and* the great mistake!

Showing Agreement and Disagreement

It is important to set up structures in your room for how students show agreement and disagreement. We use two hand signals to show these feelings. When students agree with one another, they make the shape of a Y with their hands (middle three fingers down, thumb and pinky pointing out). They point their thumb at themselves and their pinky at the person they agree with, shaking it between them. In American Sign Language, this sign means "same as you." By using this sign, students show that they are connecting with their classmate and are thinking similarly.

Showing disagreement can be more difficult. Many teachers use thumbs-up and thumbs-down signs for agreement and disagreement. While thumbs-up signs work great for agreement and can be encouraging, looking around the room and seeing lots of thumbs-down signs can be very discouraging. Other teachers like to use the phrase "I respectfully disagree" to show disagreement. It is important to keep a positive connotation associated with the word *disagreement*. You can also encourage students to say they are "thinking differently." The visual symbol for "thinking differently" or "disagreeing respectfully" is tapping your pointer finger on your forehead (brain). For a child who is sharing, it is much more encouraging to look around and see students tapping their brains instead of a sea of thumbs-down signs.

Practicing Disagreement with Written Tasks

Disagreements can also be encouraged through mathematical tasks that present two arguments for an answer or way of thinking. The student's job is to then choose which argument they agree or disagree with and justify their thinking. Practicing these disagreements on paper can help students develop the conversation skills necessary for oral disagreement. These problems are also great for discussing mathematical mistakes with the class. Some examples of these types of problems are listed below.

Disagreement Task with One Correct and One Incorrect Answer	Disagreement Task in Which Both Sides Are Correct
Mariana and Valerie are both subtracting 89 from 126. Mariana thinks the answer is 43. Valerie thinks the answer is 37. Who do you agree with, and why?	*Elliot and Hunter are trying to show the number 24 on a tens and ones mat. Elliot showed 24 using 2 tens and 4 ones. Hayes showed 24 using 1 ten and 14 ones. They are having an argument about who is correct. Who do you agree with, and why?*

BEING BRAVE WITH NEW STRATEGIES

It is not unusual for students to get stuck using one particular strategy. They find a strategy, tool, or model that works for them and begin to use it for every problem-solving task, sometimes even if it doesn't make sense. Students need to continually expand their strategy bank, learning and developing higher-efficiency, deeper-level strategies. In order to do this, students must feel confident enough to try out new strategies they may not feel comfortable with. As teachers, we must encourage students to be brave with trying new things.

One way to encourage new strategy use is through precise praise. When a student comes up with a new strategy, uses a new tool, or thinks about something in a different way, make a big deal out of it! Have them share their thinking with the class and openly praise them for their novel idea or for trying something different. Continuing to acknowledge students for this throughout the year allows students to understand that new and different thinking is valued. They will then begin to push themselves to be brave with new strategies.

The vast majority of students like sharing their thinking with the class. As teachers, we use this motivation to encourage students to use new tools or strategies. After introducing a problem task to students, before they begin working on the task, we choose to be more specific about what we will be looking for as we choose students to share that day. For example, we may say, "Today as you work, I will be looking for students who choose to use a new strategy to solve the problem and asking them to share with the class," or "Today, I will be looking for students who use different strategies to solve the problem."

If you want students to start using a new tool that they haven't tried yet, introduce the problem and point out the novel tool to the students. Say, "Today I'll be looking for students to share who try using base ten blocks to solve the problem." Even if students are unfamiliar with the tool, they will begin making use of it on their own through exploration or trial and error.

A note of caution: it is important that you do not specify which tool to use every day. This should be an occasional strategy to use to introduce a new tool or push students toward a more efficient strategy. If you specify a tool or strategy to use every day, you run the risk of telling students how to solve the problem and taking away the freedom to choose.

Another way to introduce a new tool is to give students free time to explore with the tool in an unstructured way prior to using it. As a whole class, students can share some of the observations and discoveries they made while using the tool. Posing questions such as, "I wonder what type of problem this tool could be used for?" can deepen their thinking about a new tool.

When Things Don't Seem to Be Working

What do I do when a student is afraid of making mistakes?

Sometimes, no matter how much time you spend reinforcing the idea that mistakes are valued and praised, a student will still be fearful of making mistakes. Some students may hesitate to complete, or even start, a problem if they aren't sure they'll get the answer right. These students require much more encouragement and reinforcement from the teacher. Begin with a conversation about why they may be afraid of making mistakes, and continue to remind them daily that even if they get the answer wrong, the process of trying to find the answer helps them learn! Encourage them to try any strategy that they are comfortable with to solve a problem. When they make a mistake and learn from it, celebrate it privately with the student, but think carefully before you have them share this mistake with a larger group. Sometimes students may be encouraged by cheers from their classmates, but others may be embarrassed and this could further deter them from risk-taking in the future.

It may also be helpful to connect with the student's family if they are overly fearful. You may need to encourage parents to understand the value of mistakes. By aligning the messages received from adults at school and those received from adults at home, we increase the chance that these students will develop mathematical confidence. While we may not always be able to control what is happening at home, reaching out and making connections with families may help you understand where some of these fears stem from and can potentially change the way math is approached at home.

It may also be helpful to reframe language in the classroom for a student who is afraid of making mistakes. Instead of pointing out a mistake, you might say, "Would you like to revise your thinking here?" As writers, we revise our work to more clearly communicate our ideas. In math, we revise our thinking as we learn new concepts and hear the ideas of others. By "revising thinking," we take the pressure off mistake-making.

What do I do when a student isn't taking risks?

If a student gets stuck on one particular strategy and seems to be resistant to taking risks with new strategies, you may need to spend some time working with this student on using different tools and strategies. After launching a problem task, check in with this student first. You might guide the student to a different strategy by saying something like, "I noticed that you've been using counters to solve problems for the last few days. Do you think you could try a new tool, like a number line, today?" If the student is still hesitant, you can persist by saying, "Let's try the number line first, and then you can check your work with counters to see if it worked." By checking with the more comfortable strategy, the student will begin to see that a new strategy works to get to the same answer but may be more efficient.

If students are working in pairs or groups, you can also pair this student with someone who is using a different strategy. Encourage the student partner to explain their strategy to the hesitant student, and have them work together to solve the problem.

You can also encourage the student with growth-mindset language. "Let's challenge your brain today by using a different strategy!" When the student does try a new strategy, celebrate! Praise them for being brave with a new idea and growing their brain. Invite them to share their strategy with the class and encourage the class to congratulate them for being brave with their new strategy choice. Heap the praise upon them and then catch them doing it again!

What do I do when a student doesn't want to share?

In primary grades, it is rare that students do not want to share, but it may happen. It is much more common in intermediate grades for students to be hesitant to share their ideas with the class. There could be multiple reasons for this: students might be shy, unconfident, or worried about looking bad in front of their friends. Whatever the reason, we need to encourage these students to be brave and share with the class.

One way to do this is to remind them that good mathematicians need to be able to share their thinking with others. What if the greatest mathematicians and scientists didn't share their thinking? We would never know of all their wonderful discoveries!

You might also point out that no one else in the class used the strategy that they used, if this is the case. "No one else has used this strategy, and you could really teach the class a great deal about fractions by sharing this strategy with them!" or "I would be so sad if the other students couldn't hear your wonderful ideas, because I really think they could learn from them."

Give shy students a fair amount of advance notice before they need to get up in front of the group. This will give them a chance to think through what they would like to say. Suggest that they practice what they are going to share with a partner or whisper it to the wall or a stuffed animal. If you have a microphone system set up in your classroom, it may be helpful to use it with students. They won't have to worry about projecting their voice and then can simply focus on getting out what they need to say.

Students may also be English learners or have language difficulties that hold them back from sharing. It is important to provide structures that allow these students to share their thinking in a safe way. For example, students could have a partner help them share—they may point or gesticulate toward parts of their own thinking on their paper while a partner explains orally. As the teacher, you can also have a student show their thinking to the class while you point out what they showed on their papers to justify their thinking. Sentence frames for ELLs can also provide the structure they may need to share ideas. You can even use a language translation app in which ELLs talk into your device in their home language and the app translates into English for them. Then you can celebrate how this student shared their ideas and also taught the class a little about their own language.

One final consideration to keep in mind is that in some cultures, it may not be considered appropriate for some people to speak in public. Keeping this in mind can be helpful as you try different strategies to encourage a student to be comfortable with sharing, especially when trying to understand why a student may be hesitant to share.

What do I do when a student makes a mistake on purpose to share?

Sometimes, once you begin celebrating student mistakes, a few students take it to the extreme and begin intentionally "making mistakes" so they can share their thinking with the class. This happens most often with primary students who enjoy public attention and praise. With these students, a direct one-on-one conversation may be necessary. Point out to the student that when we make mistakes on purpose, this does not help us grow and challenge our brains.

A discussion of honesty may also be necessary. Emphasize that as students are working, you expect them to honestly communicate their strategies for solving the problem. You can relate this to scientific reporting. If scientists misrepresent their ideas or thinking, they are discredited! Mathematicians need to honestly share their ideas and develop trusting relationships with their fellow mathematicians. Make it clear that in your classroom you expect and respect honesty, and that when students accurately record and explain their thinking, they will be given opportunities to share.

What do I do when a student gives up or complains that math is too hard?

This a common problem across grade levels. Students with low math confidence will easily give up when confronted with challenging tasks. These students need continual reminders of how our brains work and how we learn. Say things such as, "If it wasn't challenging, you wouldn't be learning!" or "If it was easy, I wouldn't be doing my job to help you learn!" Catch moments when these students attempt strategies or persevere through a problem. Celebrate these moments and praise students for continuing through a challenging problem. This is a great time to bring in the use of the word *yet*.

A deep conversation about perseverance may be necessary. Ask students, "If we give up because it seems too hard, how will we learn it?" The only way to learn something new is to keep trying and keep practicing. You may want to take some more time to relate this to someone the child admires. If LeBron James had given up when basketball practice got too hard, would he have been as great a basketball player as he became?

It's important to remember, though, that if a student is getting overly frustrated, this may be a signal that the math *is* too hard. Use formative assessments to determine students' mathematical understanding, and provide problems that stretch their thinking, but not too much. Giving a student a math problem that is above their zone of proximal development will only frustrate and anger them. Give students problems that appropriately challenge their skills, differentiating as needed to make sure that all students have the right level of challenge.

Summary

In order for students to be successful mathematicians, they need to be able to persevere through challenging problems, embrace and learn from mistakes, and take risks with trying new and different ideas. You can increase your students' mathematical confidence through strategic read-alouds and videos, self-evaluation, and careful praise. Be conscious of the specific language you are using in the classroom during math time, and be deliberate in reinforcing the use of this language. Encourage mistake-making, and remind students that in learning from these mistakes, we become stronger mathematicians. By setting up a community where students feel comfortable and confident, you are setting them up for success with mathematics.

Chapter Four Great Minds Think Differently

BELIEFS

6 There are different strategies for solving a problem.

7 It's not just about the answer.

One of the biggest challenges in implementing a problem-solving-based classroom is the belief that there is only one right way to do math. For many years, math has been a procedural subject: learn the algorithm, memorize the facts, follow the steps, and get the answer. Sense making has played a very small role. Math, however, isn't just calculation; it is a balance of procedural fluency, conceptual understanding, and problem-solving (including strategic competence, adaptive reasoning, and productive disposition) (NCTM 2014). For years, we've emphasized the importance of computation and procedure while ignoring conceptual understanding, problem-solving, and a student's general mindset about math.

By encouraging students to flexibly use a variety of strategies when problem-solving, we help them develop the skills and confidence necessary to choose and use an appropriate strategy given the context of a particular problem. Students can then gain a deeper understanding of numbers and mathematical concepts by explaining their thinking and making sense of the problem on their own. Those who can clearly communicate and reason about mathematics have a greater potential for understanding the concepts that underlie the problems.

Multiple Strategies and Justification: Why They Matter

To change the way we and our students think about math, it is important to emphasize two key beliefs:

- There are different strategies to solve a problem, and students should be flexible in using a variety of strategies.
- While finding the answer is the end goal, it's more important to be able to explain how we got there.

When students are able to explain their thinking and have freedom to pick a strategy that works for them, they are able to create meaning around mathematical concepts.

MULTIPLE STRATEGIES

Students deepen their conceptual understanding by seeing and using a variety of strategies. When exposed to many strategies and representations, students learn to pick the strategy that not only makes the most sense but is also the most efficient given a particular problem. Students also need to spend time comparing different strategies and making connections between multiple representations of a problem, strengthening their mathematical understanding as they do. As teachers, we must create a classroom culture that empowers students to try new strategies and bravely compare those strategies with those of their classmates.

JUSTIFICATION

Teaching students to focus not just on the answer but on the process of getting to the answer (and the need to be able to explain that process to others) helps students clarify their thinking, communicate it to others, and make connections between their own thinking and the thinking of others. John A. Van de Walle et al. (2014, 6) say that when students focus on the process, they "develop their understanding of mathematics because they are at the center of explaining, providing evidence or justification, finding or creating examples, generalizing, analyzing, making predictions, applying concepts, representing ideas in different ways, and articulating connections or relationships between the given topic and other ideas." Students gain a deeper understanding of numbers and mathematical concepts through the act of explaining their thinking because they are able to make sense of the problem on their own.

Teachers can also use these representations and justifications for assessment purposes. When we look at students' representations of their thinking, we can see the students' level of understanding as well as any areas where students have misconceptions.

Encouraging Multiple Strategies and Justification

Teaching students to make use of multiple strategies and to represent and justify their thinking instead of just writing an answer can be challenging and takes time. It requires constant reinforcement, along with questioning from the teacher and other students as their skills develop. At the beginning of the year, students realize quickly that they are not going to be able to put down an answer and be done with math for the day. From there, the hard work begins. It is our job to encourage students to believe in themselves as mathematicians so they feel comfortable sharing, discussing, and explaining strategies.

CLASSROOM STRUCTURES

In the first days of school, we see students who write down one giant number for their answer and with a grin from ear to ear drop their pencil and say, "I'm done!" The grin soon disappears when you ask, "How do you know?" Many students, especially students who are used to always getting the right answer and being praised for it, freeze when you ask them how they got their answer. There are several things teachers can do to reinforce the importance of multiple strategies and justification.

Tasks That Elicit Thinking

In order to elicit valuable student explanation in math, the tasks or problems we give children have to be meaningful. John A. Van de Walle et al. (2014, 18) say that it is the teacher's responsibility to expose children to problems that "support the development of the mathematical ideas you want children to learn." Students will develop deeper understanding of a concept by applying it to a relevant, real-world context.

Look at the following place value tasks:

Problem A	Problem B
How many tens and ones are in the number 37?	*Anna was cleaning her room on Saturday and she needed to organize all her books. She has 37 books and wants to put 10 books in each tub. How many tubs will Anna need? Will she have any books left over? Please justify your thinking.*

Both problems relate to base ten concepts, but the problems are quite different with regard to the thinking and understanding required to solve them. Chances are that a student solving Problem A will look to the digit and its place and easily say, "3 tens and 7 ones." Although understanding that the place of a digit will determine the number's value is an important concept, it's hard to tell if the student has a true understanding. Problem B allows students to think at a deeper level and use strategies or tools that make sense to them. By analyzing the strategies a student may have used to solve Problem B, we can see what understanding the student does have.

Some other examples of tasks that provide opportunities for justifications include

- a disagreement in math in which students need to explain who is correct and why
- a task that requires students to explain mathematical reasoning to someone else

With any of these tasks, we ask students to justify their answers by responding to questions such as, "How do you know?" and "Why did you use that strategy?" These questions should be asked daily and repeatedly. When we ask students to explain how they know, we take the focus off the answer and place it on the strategy and reasoning. When students can explain why they chose a strategy, we reinforce that there are multiple ways to solve a problem and one isn't better than another.

Explaining mathematical reasoning works well with more procedural tasks, such as using a ruler or other measurement tools. For example, "The kindergarteners are having trouble with telling time. Can you write a letter explaining how to tell the time on an analog clock to help the kindergarteners?" or "Explain to your second-grade friend how to measure the height of a new book to see if it fits on your shelf. Use inches on a ruler for your measurement."

Student Shares

Students will typically show their thinking in a variety of ways. It is important to expose students, through student sharing, to the full variety of strategies that you see being used regularly in your classroom. At the beginning, we look for students who have an organized way of explaining their thinking and who are able to articulate the steps they have taken to solve the problem. Then we have these children share their learning with the class. It is through these student shares that they are able to teach their classmates new strategies and ways to explain their thinking on the paper.

During the share, we also ask students to explain each others' thinking or strategies in their own words to reinforce listening skills and ensure they understand strategies. The share allows for students to see similarities and differences between each other's strategies and make meaningful connections.

We also encourage children to justify their thinking while sharing. Students are given the opportunity to answer questions posed by their classmates and the teacher. In answering questions, they can defend and justify what they have done to solve the problem. Just like in reading, we teach students to refer back to the text of the problem to justify why they took certain steps in solving it.

Consider the following vignette in which Ms. Kaplan facilitates a strategy share with this addition problem: "Max was walking through the park. He saw 2 squirrels in a tree. 5 squirrels joined them. How many squirrels are in the tree now?" Scarlett, a first grader, is sharing her strategy as the class is gathered on the carpet. She shows her work on the document camera (see Figure 4.1).

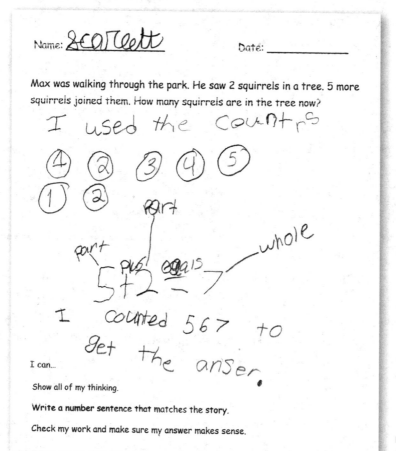

Name: Scarlett Date: ____________

Max was walking through the park. He saw 2 squirrels in a tree. 5 more squirrels joined them. How many squirrels are in the tree now?

I used the countrs

(4) (2) (3) (4) (5)

(1) (2)

part

part

whole

plus equals

5+2=7

I counted 5 6 7 to get the anser.

I can...

Show all of my thinking.

Write a number sentence that matches the story.

Check my work and make sure my answer makes sense.

Figure 4.1: Scarlett's Paper

Scarlett: *First I drew 5 circles and then 2 more. Then I counted 5, 6, 7 and I got 7 squirrels.*

Ms. Kaplan: *Thank you, Scarlett. Would someone like to tell us how Scarlett solved the problem in your own words? Bennett?*

Bennett: *First, she drew the circles for 5 and 2. Then she counted on from 5 and got 7 squirrels.*

Ms. Kaplan: *Thumbs-up if you understand Scarlett's strategy.* [pauses for think time] *I see some sideways thumbs. Can we ask a question to help us understand? Stephanie?*

Stephanie: *Why did you start counting from 5?*

Scarlett: *Because 5 is the bigger number and it's easier to count on from.*

In this vignette, Scarlett was able to clearly articulate her strategy and justify her thinking. Bennett was able to explain his strategy in his own words, and when Stephanie didn't understand, she asked a question to clarify. Ms. Kaplan simply facilitated conversation without explaining, justifying, or praising student ideas.

Ways to Share

It is important to discuss different ways that we can show and explain thinking. Start by brainstorming with students what a good justification might include. The specifics may vary depending on the grade level and experience of your students. Pictures and basic modeling with circles are a common go-to at the primary grades in the beginning of the year. As students develop understanding of more complex concepts, they will be able to use words, symbols, equations, and more complex models like number lines, bar models, or area models. Revisit these discussions throughout the year as students develop new ideas.

Here are some ways to have students share their strategies:

- Invite students who used manipulatives such as cubes, counters, or place value blocks to bring their manipulatives to a document camera and show what they did. Eventually you can encourage students to draw representations of these concrete models.
- Ask students who drew pictures to display those pictures under a document camera or, if the group is small enough so that everyone can see, display them directly.
- Encourage students who used an abstract model to represent a problem to explain and label the parts of their model. Likewise, set the expectation that students who use equations should be able to explain and label what the different parts of the equation represent.
- In primary grades, facilitate sharing by reading written explanations for younger students if students' invented spellings are difficult for other students to read.

When introducing a new way to show thinking, be careful of touting one way as "better" than another. Accept and encourage all strategies for solving a problem and models for representing those strategies.

Public Records

Creating a public record, or poster, that lists students' suggestions of ways to show their thinking helps hold students accountable for justifying thinking (see Figure 4.2). (These records are similar to the anchor charts commonly used in reading instruction.) We post our public records in an area of the room where children can refer to them daily. As students come up with new ideas, strategies, and models, they are added to the public record. These public records should be living, breathing documents for the classroom. Be sure to include the names of the students who develop the strategies on your chart. This gives the students ownership over their strategies and they love to see their names up there. Once you begin adding names, the students will always remind you if you forget!

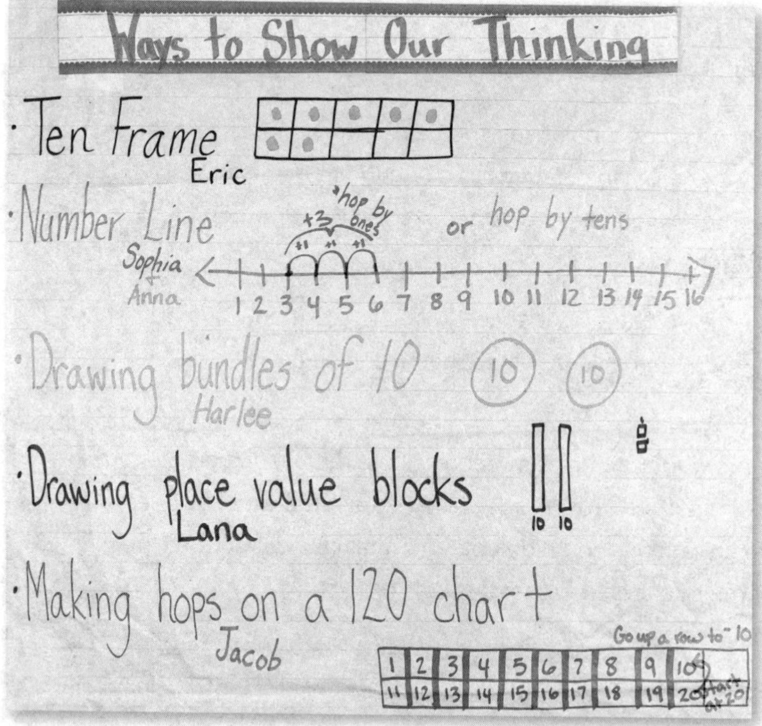

Figure 4.2: "Ways to Show Our Thinking": First-Grade Public Record

Another type of public record is a chart showing the daily problem task with student models and strategies, which is created as students share (see Figure 4.3). While students are sharing, the teacher is at the easel creating a public record that shows exactly what the students did.

One way that we encourage students to clearly state the exact steps they took to solve a problem is to pretend that we can't see their paper as they share their thinking with the class. While we re-create the student's thinking on the daily public record, we ask clarifying questions to ensure we draw the thinking correctly. For example, if a student says, "I started by drawing circles," we pause and ask, "How many circles did you draw?" As students get used to these types of questions, they begin to more precisely explain their thinking and the steps they've taken to solve the problem. Once they are precisely explaining their thinking, the teacher can ask more focused questions about the "why" of a student's strategy instead of the "what." Instead of asking, "How many circles?" we might ask, "Why did you draw that many circles?"

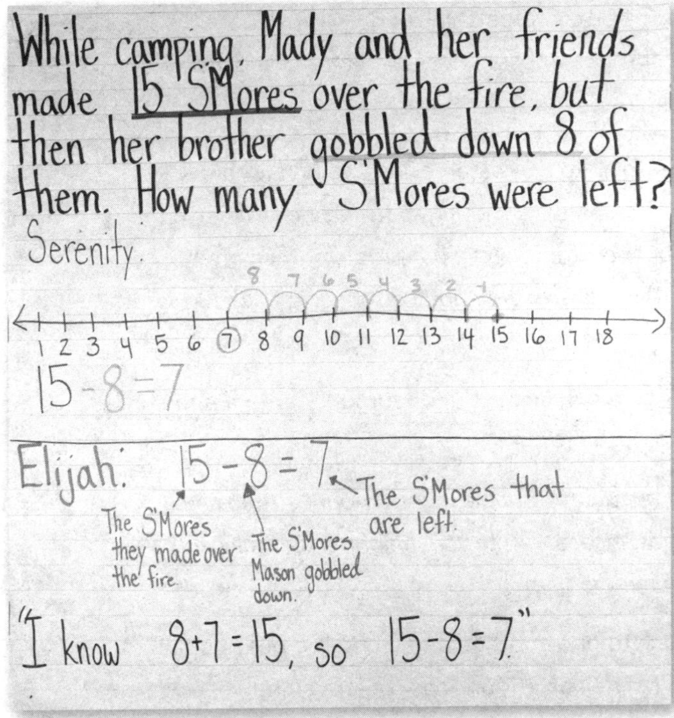

Figure 4.3: Mady's S'mores Public Record: Public Record with Student Thinking

REFLECTING ON THINKING

To teach students how to clearly explain their thinking, we encourage them to use words, numbers, and pictures or models. For example, if a student uses a number line as a model to explain their strategy to solve the problem, we ask them to record the number line and show all the steps they took to get their solution on their paper. We often use sentence frames such as "First I ______, next I _______, then I ________" to encourage them to explain the exact steps they took to solve the problem. We also ask students to label the parts of their models and strategies. A partner or teacher should be able to look at a student's paper and tell exactly how they solved the problem.

Students should be able to assess their own thinking so that they learn to choose more efficient strategies and develop more thorough justifications. To encourage this we teach students to "read thinking," evaluate the efficiency of their strategies, and self-assess their justifications.

Reading Thinking

How do we help students understand what makes an explanation effective? One option is to teach students to "read" their classmates' thinking.

In Ms. Kaplan's classroom, she has chosen two students to show their work for the problem about Max's squirrels.

> Ms. Kaplan: *Today we are going to play a game. Instead of having our classmates share their strategies, we are going to take a look at their papers and see if we can figure out how they solved the problem. Then after we guess, we can check to see if we were right! Leo is going to show his work first.*
>
> Leo puts his work (see Figure 4.4) under the document camera and steps to the side, silently.
>
> Ms. Kaplan: *Leo, remember to put a bubble in your mouth so you aren't tempted to help us! Friends, please turn to your neighbor and tell each other how you think Leo solved the problem.*
>
> The students turn and talk to one another, and when the buzz begins to die down, Ms. Kaplan calls their attention with a silent signal.

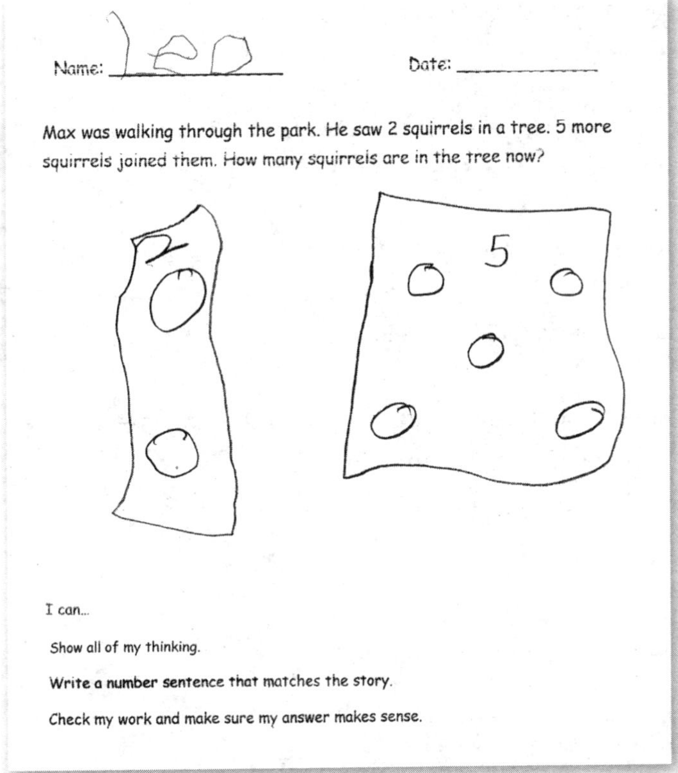
Name: Leo Date: ____________

Max was walking through the park. He saw 2 squirrels in a tree. 5 more squirrels joined them. How many squirrels are in the tree now?

2

5

I can...

Show all of my thinking.

Write a number sentence that matches the story.

Check my work and make sure my answer makes sense.

Figure 4.4: Leo's Paper

Ms. Kaplan: *Okay, can anyone tell us how they think Leo solved the problem? Theia?*

Theia: *He drew 2 circles and 5 circles, but I don't know how many he got total.*

Ms. Kaplan: *I'm seeing a lot of "I agree" signals. Would someone else like to share? Paula?*

Paula: *I agree with Theia. I don't know how he solved the problem because he just showed circles. Did you use cubes or counters?*

Leo: [unable to hold back answering] *I used counters and put them together.*

Paula: *So are the circles supposed to be counters?*

Leo: *Yes.*

Ms. Kaplan: *What could Leo do next time to show us that he used counters and put them together to solve the problem?*

The conversation continues as students brainstorm ways for Leo to show his thinking more clearly next time. After the students are finished giving advice to Leo, Ms. Kaplan has the class thank him for sharing and they celebrate his work as a great mistake that allowed the class to learn.

Next, Penelope places her paper (see Figure 4.5) under the document camera, and Ms. Kaplan reminds her to put a bubble in her mouth.

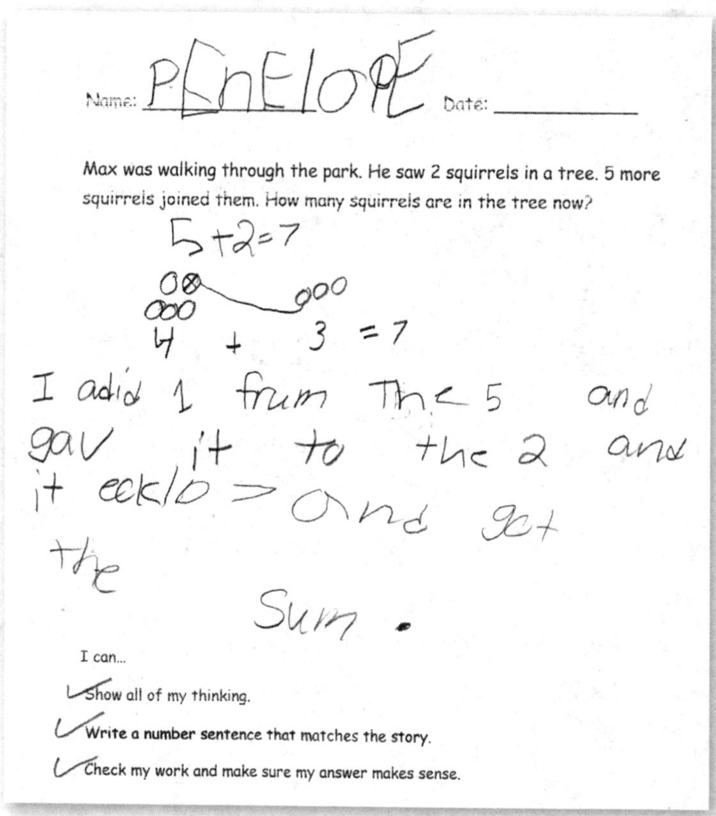

Name: PENELOPE Date: ________

Max was walking through the park. He saw 2 squirrels in a tree. 5 more squirrels joined them. How many squirrels are in the tree now?

5+2=7

4 + 3 = 7

I adid 1 frum The 5 and gav it to the 2 and it ecklo = and get the Sum.

I can...

✓ Show all of my thinking.

✓ Write a number sentence that matches the story.

✓ Check my work and make sure my answer makes sense.

Figure 4.5:
Penelope's Paper

Ms. Kaplan: *I'll read what Penelope's words say for you before we guess what she did to solve the problem. Penelope wrote, "I added 1 from the 5 and gave it to the 2 and it equaled 7 and got the sum." Now turn to your neighbor and tell each other how you think Penelope solved the problem.*

Again, Ms. Kaplan gives the students time to talk and calls their attention back to the front with a silent signal.

Ms. Kaplan: *Would anyone like to guess how Penelope solved the problem? Zev?*

Zev: *She used a fact she knows to help her!*

Ms. Kaplan: *What do you mean?*

Zev: *She changed 2 + 5 into 3 + 4. I can see in her circles, she crossed one out from the 5 and gave it to the 2.*

Ms. Kaplan: *Oh, I see. Do you think 3 + 4 is a fact Penelope knows in a snap?*

Zev: *Yes.*

Ms. Kaplan: *Show Zev if you agree. I see lots of agreement. Penelope, is this how you solved the problem?*

Penelope nods her head vigorously while smiling widely.

Ms. Kaplan: *Why do you think it was easier for us to figure out how Penelope solved the problem?*

The class begins to discuss all the ways Penelope showed her work on the paper, including the model and her explanation with words.

When you first try this technique in the classroom, students are often excited when they can "guess" their classmate's thinking just by looking at the paper. The students who share are encouraged when their classmates are able to understand exactly how they solved the problem.

However, a culture in which mistakes are welcomed and valued is critical for this activity. Early in the year, when that culture is still developing, you will need to carefully choose students who already have a growth mindset about mistakes (see Chapter 3).

Evaluating Efficiency

Students not only need to learn to explain their strategies but also need to learn to evaluate them for effectiveness and efficiency. Often, students find one model or strategy that works and then want to use that model or strategy for all problems. This is a problem for multiple reasons, the main one being that the strategy may not work for all problems. A more convoluted issue is that of efficiency. When students first start learning multiplication, it may make sense for them to draw out each group and put an equal number of dots in each group using repeated addition. However, after developing a deeper understanding of multiplication, we would expect students to move on to more abstract strategies such as open arrays and derived facts. After students have become confident with their explanations, models, and sharing, it is important to begin teaching students how to evaluate the efficiency of strategies. It is through this evaluation that you can push your students to higher-level strategies.

Imagine that most of your students used a direct modeling strategy for the problem about Max's squirrels mentioned earlier. It is essential to honor where these children are, so you choose Vivian to share this strategy. You also notice that Stanley used a counting on strategy, so you choose Stanley to share his thinking with the class as well. Vivian shares first, followed by Stanley.

While students are questioning, discussing, and working to understand each strategy, introduce the term *efficiency*. Efficiency can be defined as "quick and accurate." *Quick* because good mathematicians aim to solve math problems in the quickest way they can, and *accurate* because good mathematicians don't try to work so fast that they make simple mistakes and get the answer wrong (this is one place where the importance of the right answer does come into play!). Help guide your students to the conclusion that while both strategies get us to the correct answer, Stanley's strategy is more efficient because it is much quicker.

Assessing Explanations

We also want to encourage students to assess their own progress as thinkers, explainers, and users of multiple strategies. One way to do this is with a checklist of questions or ideas that students can use to reflect on their work. You can generate such a list in a

> *There is an important balance to strike as a teacher when holding these efficiency evaluation discussions. While we are ranking strategies as to which is most efficient, we are still telling the class that one strategy is not "better" than another; both strategies are valid and can be used to get the right answer. It is also important to point out to children that efficiency shouldn't outweigh understanding. We always end an efficiency discussion with a reminder and a caution. We remind students that we want to push ourselves to choose the most efficient strategies, but we caution students that we shouldn't be choosing strategies we don't understand or don't feel we are ready for yet just because the class has decided they are more efficient. Some students may feel ready to use a strategy like Stanley's, but other students may still need those connecting cubes. This is another opportunity to reinforce the growth mindset and discuss how our brains are all different. We might not understand the most efficient strategy yet, but we'll get there soon, especially because we know it's there to use later!*

discussion with students, asking "What does good math work look like?" Sample items could include

- Did I show all my thinking on the paper?
- Did I show how I used a math tool to help me solve the problem?
- Did I label my numbers?

We sometimes add a checklist to the papers we give students, so they are reminded to justify their thinking each time (see Figure 4.6).

A self-assessment rubric is another way to encourage students to justify and show their work on their papers. Create a rubric with the students that specifies expectations for "completed" work. Notice in Figure 4.7 that the expectation is to "write the answer," not to "write the *correct* answer."

Learning to give good feedback also helps students reinforce these beliefs with each other. After students work for a bit, have them switch papers with a partner. Ask partners to read the thinking of their classmate and see if it is clear. Teach your students to give

1.NBT.2 (a) and 1.NBT.3

Name: Blessing Date: __________

Mrs. Natali was organizing the library and she found 14 **nonfiction** books. After that, she found a tub of 10 **fiction** books and 5 more **fiction** books on the shelf. Did Mrs. Natali find more fiction or nonfiction books in the library?

** Please justify your thinking*

15 > 14

14 fourteen non fiction

15 fifteen Fiction

I can....

☑ Show all of my thinking.

☑ Check my work.

☑ Write a number sentence or inequality that matches the story.

Figure 4.6: Self-Assessment Checklist

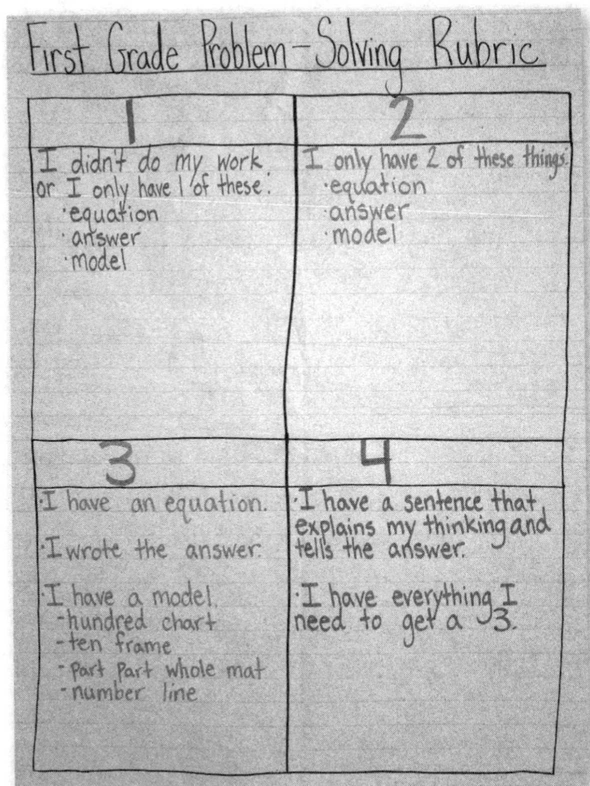

First Grade Problem-Solving Rubric
1
I didn't do my work or I only have 1 of these:
·equation
·answer
·model
2
I only have 2 of these things:
·equation
·answer
·model
3
·I have an equation.
·I wrote the answer.
·I have a model.
-hundred chart
-ten frame
-Part Part whole mat
-number line
4
·I have a sentence that explains my thinking and tells the answer.
·I have everything I need to get a 3.

Figure 4.7: First-Grade Problem-Solving Rubric

constructive feedback to one another about how to improve their representations or improve their efficiency. You can provide conversational sentence frames such as these:

> *"I see that you showed me __________, but I'm not sure where __________ is."*
>
> *"I understand where this number came from, but I'm not sure how you got this number."*
>
> *"I understand how you started, but what did you do [next/last]?"*
>
> *"Is this the most efficient strategy you could use?"*

Over time, students learn the expectations for representing their own thinking clearly on paper. When they can self-assess and critique their own thinking through rubrics and checklists, they'll be able to transfer this knowledge and begin respectfully critiquing the thinking of others—another critical mathematical skill!

When Things Don't Seem to Be Working

What do I do when a student is not using an efficient strategy or uses the same strategy every day?

Often, students will get stuck on one favorite strategy. They try to use the strategy in every problem situation, even when they are more than ready to progress to a higher-level strategy. When this happens, have a one-on-one discussion with this student during their independent time. Suggest that they try a new strategy and be explicit with naming the new strategy.

While it is important that students discover and use strategies on their own, sometimes we need to directly teach a strategy. For example, if a student is stuck on using manipulatives and counting all of them, suggest they try counting on. Directly teach how to count on, and ask the student why this may be a more efficient strategy than the one they are using. Be careful not to suggest a strategy they are not yet ready to understand. Push the student out of their comfortable strategy, but not so far that they get frustrated or lose conceptual understanding.

Another option for a student like this is to allow them to use their favorite strategy, but then suggest a "challenge" after they have solved the problem. Ask them to solve the problem using a different strategy. Presenting this request as a challenge often motivates students to try new and different strategies. You might also pair the student with another student who is more comfortable with the new strategy, so that the two can work together to compare the strategies.

Be sure to praise the student when they independently choose to use a new strategy. This will help reinforce the use of new strategies and motivate the student to independently try out new strategies.

What do I do when a student is struggling to explain an answer?

When a student is struggling to explain an answer, start by talking through the problem with the child. Start by asking what we know and what we are trying to figure out in the problem. If they are struggling to explain, go back into the text of the problem and highlight the important information and the question. Have them retell the story orally, act it out with them, or have them draw a picture.

If the student seems to understand the problem but still can't articulate how they solved it, ask procedural questions. Some examples include

"What did you do [first/next/last]?"

"What did you use to solve the the problem?"

"How could you show that on your paper?"

Ask probing questions to pull more details out of the child. For instance, if they say, "I counted," ask, "What number did you start at?" or "Did you count up or back?" or "What did your counting sound like?" You want to ask as many questions as you can to clarify ideas for the student. This may seem intimidating at first, but if you have established your questioning norms (discussed in Chapter 5), the students will feel comfortable with this type of questioning. It usually only takes one or two questioning sessions like this before students learn to explain their thinking more clearly.

Sometimes students are able to successfully use strategies but struggle to explain them clearly on their paper. When this happens, look at the work they have recorded and ask follow-up questions that push them to explain more clearly:

> *"I see you have a group of 2 circles over here, but I'm not sure what those are. How can you show me what those circles represent?"*
>
> *"I see that you used 5 x 5 to help you solve 5 x 6, but I'm not sure how it helped. How is 5 x 5 related to 5 x 6?"*

It can also be helpful to post sentence stems in the classroom that promote clear explanations. Some examples of sentence stems could be

> *"First I __________. Next I __________. Then I __________."*
>
> *"I used the __________ strategy because __________."*

What do I do when a student is using a strategy they don't understand?

Students will often try a strategy that they have seen during the share, but you will notice that they have some misconceptions about using that strategy or they cannot explain how it works for a certain problem. You can start by conferring with the student. Begin by praising the student for being brave with a new strategy, but then ask questions like, "Why did you use this strategy?" and "How do you know it works for this problem?" Through these questions, you can determine where the student is on the continuum toward understanding this strategy. While you don't want to discourage a student from using a particular strategy, you need to ensure that they have the support they need to understand that strategy. When working one-on-one or in a small group with this student, you can scaffold or directly teach proper use of the strategy.

Think in terms of the child's zone of proximal development. If a strategy is above their conceptual zone, you need to step back and provide the necessary scaffolds to get there. For example, consider this scenario. Ms. Kaplan is walking around the room after introducing a contextual problem in which students will need to add 6 + 5. She notices Elise has drawn a number line on her paper.

> **Ms. Kaplan:** *Can you tell me about this?*
>
> **Elise:** *I used a number line.*
>
> **Ms. Kaplan:** *Show me how you used it.*

Elise puts her finger on the number 6, saying "1" as she points to the 6. She continues to count on, saying "2, 3, 4, 5," and lands her final count on the number 10. Ms. Kaplan can clearly see that Elise is not understanding how to use a number line, so she asks Elise to try showing her thinking with a different strategy.

On the other hand, if a student is on the cusp of understanding an efficient strategy but just needs a little guidance, you can try partnering them with a student who is able to understand and articulate the strategy.

What do I do when a student rushes through the problem to get to the answer?

It is extremely common for children to race through the task and write one answer with no explanation, although this tendency does decrease as you reinforce the beliefs throughout the year. You will most likely be aware of the students in your class who are prone to shouting, "I'm done!" It is important to get to them early in the work time and simply ask, "How do you know?" If students cannot answer this, you can ask them to show you what they did. Then ask, "How do you think you could show that on your paper?" It is also important that you explain to the class that you are looking for someone who justified their answer to share after launching the problem to the class. The students are very eager to share and therefore tend to work hard toward that justification. A phrase we often use in our class is, "When a mathematician thinks they're done, their work has just begun." You will hear students saying this to their classmates when a student has declared, "I'm done!"

One Last Tip: Be Careful with Praise

When teachers constantly praise students for getting the right answer, the students become reliant on the teacher to tell them whether or not they are correct. We want students to look at their thinking critically, determine whether or not it makes sense, and have confidence in their own answers. Also, when we reward a student for getting the right answer, we are rewarding them for "being smart." Does that mean that tomorrow when they don't get the right answer, they are "dumb"? That is not what any of us wants them to believe, but this kind of praise can reinforce just such an impression. We treat a correct answer the same way as an incorrect one: we question it, ask for explanations, and expect evidence of thinking. We provide positive feedback to students for working hard, elaborating, justifying, clarifying, experimenting, and taking risks, not for getting the right answer. We specifically praise the work that went into the *thinking*, not the answer:

> *"I really like how you clearly showed the way you used cubes on your paper."*
>
> *"I like how you worked hard to write sentences that clearly explain the steps you took when you used the near-doubles strategy."*
>
> *"This picture shows me exactly what you did to solve the problem!"*

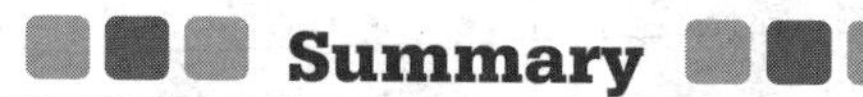

Summary

The purpose of teaching students to explain their thinking, use multiple strategies, and choose the most efficient strategy is to promote deeper understanding of mathematics and to allow students to feel like successful mathematicians as they solve problems and explain how they did it. When teaching students that math isn't just about the answer, emphasize clear thinking. Encourage clear representations with manipulatives or on paper. Praise students for working hard to show their thinking, not for coming up with the right answer. When they get the right answer, question them. When they ask you if they got the right answer, don't tell them! Ask them if they *think* the answer is correct, and why. If they tell you they think their answer is correct, ask them to prove it to you. When they are done, ask about the efficiency of their strategies.

When your students begin to pay less attention to the answer and more attention to the thinking that went into the answer, they will begin to think more critically about their own and their classmates' problem-solving. When students finally realize that getting the wrong answer isn't the end of the world, their horizons open up to allow them to experiment with different ways to solve problems and to be more flexible with how they arrive at an answer.

Chapter Five Thinking Through Questioning

BELIEFS

8 Good learners ask questions.

9 Questions from the teacher help us learn and grow.

As teachers, we encourage students to think deeply as they read, questioning an author's reasoning and motivations. We must encourage them to do the same with math. The Common Core State Standards for Mathematical Practice encourage students to provide evidence of their thinking and evaluate the evidence provided by others. One of the best ways to help students accomplish these goals is through deliberate and direct questioning, both from the teacher and by the students themselves.

Questioning: Why It Matters

Being able to ask specific, targeted questions is a skill that must be learned and practiced by both the teacher and the students. When we as teachers question students, we must learn how to ask the specific types of questions that pull out the information we are looking for from our students. As we question our students, we are also modeling effective questioning techniques. Students will learn to ask the same types of targeted questions of each other as they learn to analyze and compare their classmates' mathematical reasoning. Questioning is crucial to our math instruction.

TYPES OF QUESTIONS

Questions are one of the most valuable tools we have as teachers. Strategic, deliberate questions can push student thinking to deeper levels and open up opportunities for quick formative assessment. With every math problem we give our students, we think about which questions will allow us to formatively assess student understandings and/or misconceptions. We think about which questions will push students' thinking, allowing them to extend their understanding of mathematical concepts and ideas. As students answer questions and discuss mathematical concepts and ideas, they are able to develop a metacognitive awareness of their own understanding and thought processes.

It is also important for us as teachers to be flexible with our questioning. Even with the best-planned lesson, we can never quite know which direction a conversation may flow. Teachers must be able to adapt their questioning to the conversation as it happens. Doing this requires us to truly listen to our students and be responsive to where they are in their understanding. It requires patience and practice to become artful, thoughtful questioners.

Teacher questions generally fit into three categories:

1. *questions that clarify and probe for justification*
2. *questions that guide, challenge, and extend thinking*
3. *questions that assess understanding*

You will notice that these question types often overlap, but here we will explain the general purpose for asking each type of question. Skilled teachers must be able to choose which questions to use based on the students they are working with. In one conversation, a teacher may fluidly move back and forth between all three question purposes and types, and an individual question may address two or more purposes at once.

Questions That Clarify and Probe Thinking

Clarification questions help students understand a task, make sense of a problem, and explain their thinking more clearly. Clarification may be necessary as they solve a problem or share their thinking with others. When introducing a problem task or new idea, we use clarification questions to ensure that students understand the problem, or to help them visualize the context of the problem and help them see what the problem is asking them to figure out. Clarifying questions can also help highlight and define any new or unfamiliar vocabulary that may interfere with student understanding. Finally, clarifying questions can help ensure that the rest of the class is following along with the presenter's line of thinking during a share.

A probing question encourages students to think about the problem at a deeper level. Probing questions can also help us better understand student thinking. Both probing and clarifying questions allow us to guide students through misconceptions and help decrease obstacles that get in the way of mathematical thinking, such as reading comprehension issues or a lack of language skills. These are generally open-ended questions, allowing for multiple responses, and they should not give any clues or hints as to how to solve the problem.

The following vignette shows how we launch a problem in our classrooms and highlights the clarifying and probing questions used while introducing the task. Mrs. Dance begins by attempting to engage the students in the problem.

Mrs. Dance: *I need your help today, boys and girls. I'm having trouble with a deer in my garden and I don't know what to do. Does anybody think they know what my problem may be?*

Delaney: *The deer is eating your garden.*

Mrs. Dance: *Delaney, great prediction. Show me a private thumb if your thinking was similar to Delaney's. Well, I need you to figure out how many strawberries this deer ended up eating out of my garden. Do you think you can help me with this?*

Mrs. Dance reads the following problem at least twice: *"Mrs. Dance had 19 strawberries in her garden, but a deer came and gobbled up some strawberries. Now she has 8 strawberries left in her garden. How many strawberries did the deer eat?"*

Mrs. Dance: *What do we know about my garden?*

Julien: *The deer gobbled 8 strawberries.*

Mrs. Dance: *William, I see you're pointing to your brain, giving the "I'm thinking something different" signal. Why is that?*

Students have been taught that calling out the answer goes against the classroom expectation that everyone has the right to learn (discussed in Chapter 2). One way to prevent those who want to jump right in and answer is by leaving out the numbers in the problem or covering them with a sticky note until the problem has been discussed and visualized.

William: *The deer didn't eat 8 strawberries, but that's how many strawberries are left.*

Mrs. Dance: *Let's go back and reread the problem.*

The class chorally rereads the problem together.

Mrs. Dance: *What do we think? Did the deer eat 8 strawberries, or do I have 8 strawberries left?*

Class: *You have 8 strawberries left.*

Mrs. Dance: *What other information do we know?*

Samantha: *You had 19 strawberries at first.*

The class gives the "I agree" signal.

Mrs. Dance: *I want you to turn and talk with your math partner. What are we trying to figure out?*

Students sit knee to knee and eye to eye with their partners and discuss the question in the problem. Students are careful not to talk about how they will solve the problem or what the answer is.

Mrs. Dance [restating the task]: *What are we trying to figure out?*

Reese: *How many strawberries did the deer eat?*

Mrs. Dance: *Do we agree on the key question?*

Class: *Yes!*

Mrs. Dance: *You may use any tools you would like as you try and figure out how many strawberries this pesky deer ended up eating. I can't wait to see what you come up with as you work to solve this problem.*

Notice that during this task introduction, Mrs. Dance gave very little information to the students, other than reading and rereading the problem. She asked questions to pull the important information from the students and also encouraged the students to question one another's thinking.

Clarifying and probing questions are also used as students work to solve a problem or as they share their thinking. When one student shares, the teacher may ask questions to clarify the steps a student used in solving a problem. Clarifying questions may help students restate ideas in their own words as they listen to the thinking of their classmates.

Questions That Clarify and Probe Thinking	
During the Task Introduction	*During Work Time or Whole-Class Share*
■ What does the word ______ mean? ■ How many ______ are there? ■ Can you reread the problem? [To redirect students who seem to be misunderstanding a portion of the problem] ■ What tools can we use to solve this problem? ■ What are we trying to figure out? ■ What we do we know? ■ What is the important information? ■ Is there any information that we don't need to know? ■ How is this [different from/the same as] yesterday's task?	■ What did you do [first/next/last]? ■ How did using a ______ [model] help you solve the problem? ■ How did using that strategy help you solve the problem? ■ What tool did you use? ■ How did you know to ______ [add/subtract/multiply/divide]? ■ What in the problem told you that?

Questions That Guide, Challenge, and Extend

Questions that guide, challenge, and extend are used to push student thinking, often while creating cognitive dissonance, which increases the learning. These types of questions allow students to deepen their own reasoning as they justify their thinking. Guiding questions are also used to navigate students through misconceptions as they explain their reasoning. Additionally, they may be used to help a student get started or facilitate strategy use as students solve a problem.

Let's step back into Mrs. Dance's classroom as the kids begin to work on solving the problem introduced earlier. The students have been released from the carpet area to return to their tables and begin solving the problem. Some students go straight to their table and begin working on the problem, while others go to the math center to grab number lines, hundred charts, cubes, or another tool of their choice. Mrs. Dance walks around the room with the goal of initially targeting students who are having trouble getting started.

Marty: *I'm stuck.*

Mrs. Dance: *That's great, our brains are not working when something is easy. What are you stuck on?*

Marty: *I don't get it.*

Mrs. Dance: *Well, let's see what we know. Can you circle or underline important information as I read the problem?*

As Mrs. Dance rereads, Marty circles the 19 and the 8.

Mrs. Dance: *What did you circle?*

Marty: *19 strawberries.*

Mrs. Dance: *What does the 19 mean in the problem?*

Marty: *The strawberries you had in the beginning.*

Mrs. Dance: *What else did you circle?*

Marty: *8, because that is how many strawberries are left.*

Mrs. Dance: *Can you underline the question?*

Marty underlines the question.

Mrs. Dance: *Would you like to draw a picture of what we know or use cubes to show what is happening in the problem?*

Marty: *I want to draw a picture.*

Mrs. Dance: *I'll let you get started on your picture and come back in a few minutes to see your great work.*

Mrs. Dance continues to circle the room.

Mrs. Dance: *Julia, I see you have an 11 on your paper. What does the 11 mean?*

Julia: *That's how many the deer gobbled?*

Mrs. Dance: *How do you know it's 11? Can you tell me what you did?*

Julia: *I know you had 19 strawberries at first and then there were 8 left, so I started at 19 on the number line and hopped back to 8 and that was 11 hops.*

Mrs. Dance: *Why did you hop back on the number line?*

Julia: *Because the deer was eating your strawberries, so it's like a take-away problem.*

Mrs. Dance: *Do you think you could show all of that work on your paper and explain why you stopped at the number 8? I wonder if you could write a number sentence that matches this problem. I'll come back to see how you showed your work in a little bit.*

Mrs. Dance moves on to another student.

Mrs. Dance: *Delaney, I see you drew a picture and did a number line. Do you think one strategy is more efficient for this task?*

Delaney: *The number line because it took less time. It took me a while to draw 19 circles for the strawberries.*

Mrs. Dance: *Can you explain these two strategies to me, please?*

Delaney: *I knew it was a mystery box problem because it said "some" and we don't know how many "some" is, so I wrote 19 minus blank equals 8. First I drew 19 circles and then I crossed them out until there were 8 left like the problem said. On my number line, I started at 19 and counted back to 8 because it was subtraction and I got 11 both times.*

Mrs. Dance: *Let's pretend I had 37 strawberries. How many did the deer eat?*

During this work time, Mrs. Dance asked questions to guide students toward a strategy, to evaluate strategy efficiency, and to extend thinking. In her conversation with Marty, she used questioning to guide him toward the important information in the problem and help him choose a strategy to use. With Julia, she asked questions to push her to more clearly justify her thinking on her paper. With Delaney, she asked questions to push her thinking beyond the context of the problem by evaluating efficiency and extending her thinking with more difficult numbers.

These types of questions may also be used during whole-group discussions to guide, challenge, and extend the thinking of the class as a group. Through formative assessments, the teacher can make judgments as to which line of questioning (clarifying and probing or guiding and extending) may be best during each whole-group lesson.

Questions That Assess Understanding

Questions can be a powerful, daily formative assessment tool. By intentionally questioning students, teachers can gather important evidence of student understanding and strategy use and make informed instructional decisions about where to go next, what may need revisiting, and how to further challenge our learners.

Let's visit Mrs. Dance's room again as students are back on the carpet, sharing their thinking with the whole group. She begins by asking students to think about the problem they just solved and show a secret silent signal that reflects how they feel about their understanding of the problem. Students place a thumb down, sideways, or up on their tummies to show how solving the problem felt. A thumbs-down signal means the problem was too tricky, sideways means "I understood but didn't finish," and thumbs-up means the problem felt just right. This quick self-assessment both promotes metacognitive reflection and gives the teacher a quick overview of how students feel they understood the problem at hand.

> **Mrs. Dance:** *I'm seeing some sideways thumbs, which is awesome because our brains really had to work and grow while solving this problem. Delaney is going to share today, and I want you to pay close attention to what she says. While she is talking, decide if you agree or disagree. Please be thinking of what you did and figure out if your strategy is different from or similar to Delaney's strategies. Think of questions you might ask her about her mathematical thinking. Remember, questions show we care about her thinking and questions help our brain grow.*

Questions
That Guide, Challenge, and Extend

- How can we get started on this problem?
- Let's reread the problem. What do we know? [*When students seem to be missing information or are having trouble getting started*]
- I saw you use a 100 chart yesterday. Do you think that would help you today?
- Can you tell me more about this?
- Why did you ________?
- What does the number ___ mean in your number sentence?
- Can you use a second strategy to prove your thinking?
- What if there were 20 instead of 10?
- Does that strategy always work?
- Would this work if the numbers were different?
- What strategy is most efficient?
- Can you create a similar problem that I could give to the class?
- Why did you use ___________ to solve this problem? [*To guide students toward clearer justification or help them analyze why they chose a particular tool/strategy*]
- How is your strategy similar to ________'s strategy?
- How is your strategy different?

Delaney shares her work under the document camera while Mrs. Dance records it onto the chart paper to make a public record documenting her strategy. This will be posted on the class's math wall with other previous shares that have taken place.

Mrs. Dance: *Does anyone have questions for Delaney so far?*

Jacob: *Why did you cross out the circles?*

Mrs. Dance: *Great question, Jacob!*

Delaney: *The problem said that the deer was eating the strawberries, so I wanted to cross them off.*

Mrs. Dance: *Any other questions?*

Max: *I disagree with Delaney. I got 27 strawberries.*

Mrs. Dance: *Did anyone else get 27? Turn and talk.*

Mrs. Dance: *I'm hearing that a few of you got 27. Can someone who got 27 justify their thinking, please?*

Aaliyah: *I know that 19 plus 8 is 27, so the answer is 27.*

Mrs. Dance: *Thank you, Aaliyah. Can you call on someone who is thinking something different?*

Aaliyah calls on Jayden, who is giving a silent signal to show she is thinking differently.

Jayden: *The problem said that you had 19 and then 8 left, so 27 would not make sense for the problem.*

Mrs. Dance: *Delaney, can you explain the number sentence you have on your paper and why you wrote that?*

Delaney: *I put 19 first because that is how many strawberries were in your garden at first, and then I put a subtraction symbol because the problem said that the deer gobbled up your strawberries and so I knew it was minus. I have "blank" because I didn't know how many were gobbled by the deer, but I knew you had 8 strawberries left, so I wrote it equals 8. Then I found out that the deer had eaten 11 after I drew my picture and did my number line.*

Mrs. Dance: *Can we have two different answers for this problem? Do addition and subtraction both work? I want you to turn and talk about this.*

The students then discuss this with their partners.

Mrs. Dance: *What are we thinking?*

Aaliyah: *I revised my thinking and I don't agree with my 27 anymore; I agree with Delaney.*

Mrs. Dance: *Why?*

Aaliyah: *The deer didn't eat 19 plus 8 more strawberries, so 27 doesn't make sense.*

As Mrs. Dance facilitated this share, she was able to assess through questioning that her students were experiencing a common misconception. In this missing-part problem, many of her students were adding the two numbers together. She used questioning to guide them through this misconception and help them come to the conclusion that addition did not make sense for this problem. She listened in during turn and talks to assess what students were misunderstanding in the problem and then was able to directly address the misconception within the share.

> *Note that many good probing and challenging questions in this example came from students! We'll discuss the important role of student questions shortly.*

This type of questioning can also be used as students explore a problem on their own. You might start with questions for assessment and then choose which types of questions to ask next based on that assessment.

Questions That Assess

- Why did you start at 7?
- Tell me what this means.
- What makes you think that?
- What does the number _____ represent in the problem?
- How do you know that this works?
- Why did you use that operation?
- I saw that some of our friends had _____ as their answer. What do you think they did to get that answer?
- Why did you choose this [tool/strategy]? [*To determine whether or not a student is thinking critically about their choice of tool or strategy*]
- Which part of the problem gave you that information?

STUDENT QUESTIONING

Student questioning is just as important as teacher questioning. It enables students to advocate for their own learning and develop their own understanding

Children by nature are always asking questions, and it is our job to create an environment that nurtures and encourages these questions. Asking questions is a skill that all students need to develop to be critical, metacognitive mathematicians. In order to skillfully ask their own questions, students must be able to assess their own understanding, pinpoint where any confusions may exist or where they are feeling a lack of clarity, and choose the right question to ask in order to gather the information they need to deepen their learning. Teaching students to question themselves and one another takes time, patience, and much praise. We instill the belief in students that they learn the most by asking questions. We stress that it is very important to ask a question when there is something you don't understand, something you don't agree with, or something you are curious about.

Young learners often feel uncomfortable with the idea of questioning and feel that asking questions shows a lack of understanding, which means they are not smart. For this reason, not only must we directly teach students about the importance of asking questions, but we must also teach them how to ask meaningful questions. In the next few sections, we will first return briefly to teacher questioning, and then focus on student questioning for the rest of the chapter.

Effective Teacher Questioning

In order to be deliberate about asking meaningful questions, it is very important to think through the lesson. Solve the problem or complete the task yourself and do the math *before* you give it to your students. Consider the misconceptions students will have and predict the variety of strategies students will use. You will also want to think about what your students may say and plan questions to either clarify, guide, or extend their thinking. Appendix B shows the template we use when thinking through our lessons, but you may play around to find one that works best for you. Appendix C is this same template with guiding questions to help you as you plan a lesson. The more you think through each lesson, planning the questions you might ask, the more meaningful your questions will be and this process will soon become natural.

BUILDING STUDENTS' WILLINGNESS TO ANSWER

Not all students are immediately comfortable when a teacher questions their thinking. Some come to the classroom with the preconceived notion that when a teacher questions their work or thinking, it must mean that they are wrong. At the beginning of the year, students will often erase whatever it is they have on their paper as soon as any question is asked. When asked questions such as, "How do you know?" or "Why did you subtract?" they begin erasing away. Over the first months of the school year, it is important to emphasize the purpose of our questioning and to explain to students that when we as teachers ask questions it is because we want to understand or deepen their thinking. We must continually reassure our students that just because we are asking a question, it does not mean that they are wrong. It takes time, constant reassurance, and many reminders before students will learn to grow comfortable with teacher questioning. As with any new learning, some students take longer than others to become comfortable with this kind of questioning. However, it is worth the time, effort, and patience it takes to develop a relationship with these students so that they can trust that our questioning is not a negative judgment but simply what it is: a question.

We also encourage comfort with questioning by explaining to our students that answering and asking questions makes their brains grow stronger in math by getting them to think beyond just the correct answer. When students become more used to our questioning, they often begin to anticipate questions, answering them before they are asked. They know that when you ask them about their thinking, answers aren't enough and justification is always expected. The need to ask "How do you know?" slowly dissipates throughout the year.

Effective Student Questioning

Teaching questioning skills is not an easy process. It involves patience, scaffolding, and focused instruction.

QUESTIONS VERSUS STATEMENTS

Asking a question is not something that a lot of our students know how to do innately, especially at the primary level. At the beginning of the year, our youngest learners will often confuse statements with questions. It is important to start the year by teaching the difference between a question and a statement.

One way we do this is through the use of a question/statement T-chart. Find an engaging or interesting photograph that you know will spark the interest of your students. Show it to the class and tell them you'd like them to work with a partner to ask questions or talk about what they notice in the picture.

As a whole group, provide students with definitions of a question and a statement. A statement can be defined as something we observe, notice, or feel. A question is something that can be answered to gain more information. Make a question/statement T-chart as students share about the discussion they had with their partners. When someone shares a statement or question about the photograph, ask students to choose which column the sentence belongs in. Facilitate a discussion as students decide which sentences belong where on the chart, asking students to justify their thoughts. By charting the examples, students are able to see clearly how questions and statements differ. Leave this chart posted in the room and refer back to it as necessary throughout the year.

ACCEPT ALL QUESTIONS . . . AT FIRST

Nonmathematical questions like, "Why did you color the tree blue?" or "Why is your 9 backwards?" are not uncommon at the beginning of the year, especially in the primary grades. As students are just beginning to understand how to ask questions, it is important to accept these questions and praise students for asking them. If you begin limiting question types too soon, students may be hesitant to ask questions at all. However, as they progress in their understanding of questioning, you will eventually need to discourage this type of questioning. Explain the difference between a "mathematical question," or one that asks about the mathematical strategy or model, and a "nonmathematical question," or one that asks about spelling, handwriting, or other unrelated topics. Encourage students to ask only mathematical questions during share times.

NOTICING AND WONDERING

Another way to encourage students to ask questions is through the classroom routine "I Notice, I Wonder" suggested by the Math Forum (2017). In this routine, students are given a math problem or scenario and encouraged to first talk about what they notice in the problem. These noticings can be charted as a whole class, discussed with partners, or discussed in a small group. Then students are asked, "What do you wonder?" They should be encouraged to discuss all the things they wonder about the math problem or scenario. In this routine, students feel comfortable asking questions because they are encouraged to think about the problem in a low-stress way. They are being asked not to solve the problem but simply to wonder about it.

Once students are comfortable with this routine, teachers can take it a step further by asking students to analyze the types of noticings and wonderings they are having. Teachers can ask questions such as, "Which of our wonderings help us to understand the problem mathematically?" or "Which of the things we noticed give us information we need to solve the problem, and which do not?" By analyzing what they notice and wonder, students begin to think metacognitively about the kinds of questions they are asking.

TEACHER MODELING

Modeling is crucial when promoting student questioning. Just as we deliberately model kind and polite words with our students to encourage respectful behavior, we need to deliberately model questioning to encourage students to begin asking their own questions.

During the beginning of the year, most of the questioning in math will come from the teacher. As students share thinking during daily lessons, teachers need to be intentional in asking all types of questions. After a while, encourage your students to ask questions of one another. When you begin to hear them mimicking the types of questions you ask, use specific praise to talk about why those questions are important. As you strategically praise students for asking focused questions, more students will begin to follow suit, trying their best to ask deep-level questions. You will soon hear students using those same questions with their peers, and they will begin developing their own questions instead of just mimicking your modeled questions.

You can push the level of questioning in your classroom throughout the year by scaffolding the types of questions that you model. At the beginning of the year, ask straightforward questions such as, "Why did you choose that strategy?" or "How did that tool help you solve the problem?" Once students begin asking these questions on their own, increase the complexity of the questions you are modeling. Ask, "Why did using a number line make sense for this problem?" or "How did using an area model help you make sense of the problem?" As you increase the complexity of the questions you model, students will increase the complexity of their own questioning.

QUESTION AND CONVERSATION STEMS

Question and conversation stems can be extremely helpful in getting students, especially English learners, to ask questions and discuss mathematical concepts. Create sentence stems for students to use and post them in your room to help guide student questioning (see Figure 5.1). As students come up with other questions, add stems for them to your collection. One way to encourage students to use the stems is by writing a student's name on a sticky note and placing it on a stem when they use it (or letting them do so). The kids love to see their name up there, and you will find that kids often notice when others in the class use a stem they added.

TEACHER TALK MOVES

While there are a variety of talk moves you can use to promote mathematical discussions, a few specific moves help students develop their ability to ask questions.

Questions like, "Can you tell me more about that?" or "What did you mean when you said ______?" or "Can you say that again in a different way?" help students see that elabora-

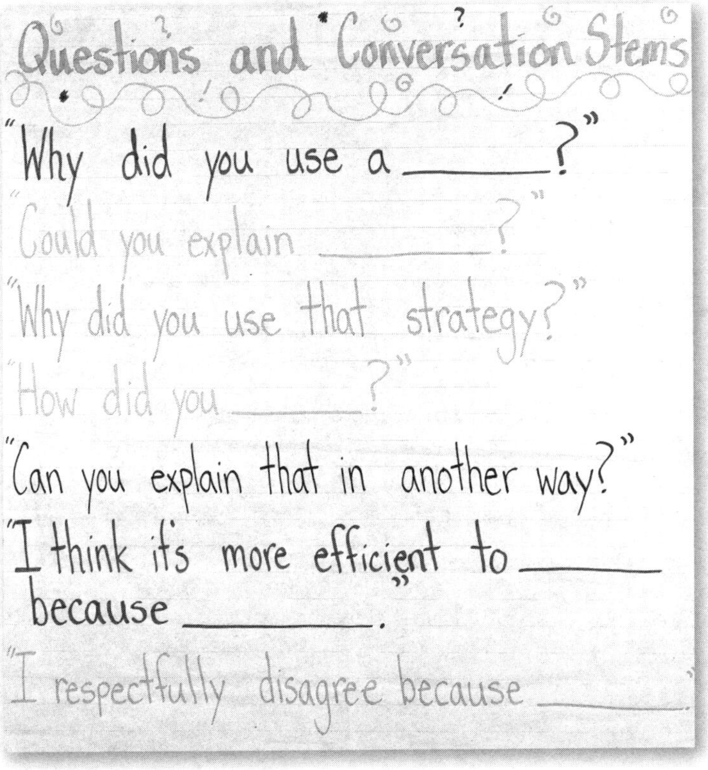

Figure 5.1: Questions and Conversation Stems

tion is sometimes necessary for better understanding. Directly modeling these types of talk moves helps them become part of the math language in your classroom, and students will begin using them during group discussions and with their peers.

During discussions, we often ask students to rephrase one another's thinking to ensure understanding and keep them engaged in the discussion. When students struggle to rephrase their classmates, encourage them to think of a question they can ask to help clarify what the student sharing is trying to say. Ask, "What questions can we ask _____ to better understand [his/her] thinking?" (For more on rephrasing, see Chapter 2.)

Another talk move that you can use frequently is simply asking students if they have any questions. You can keep it simple, asking, "Does anyone have any questions for _____?" Or you can narrow the focus by asking question like, "Does anyone have any questions for _____ about how [he/she] used the doubling and halving strategy to solve this multiplication problem?"

Teacher Talk Moves to Encourage Questioning

- Does anyone have any questions for ___________?
- Does anyone have any questions about ___________'s strategy?
- What questions can you ask ___________ to help yourself better understand [his/her] thinking?
- Talk moves to model in order to encourage student use:
  - Can you tell me more about that?
  - What did you mean when you said ___________?
  - I heard you say ___________. Is that correct?
  - Can you say that again in a different way?

PRAISE

As teachers, we know that our students will do anything and everything to please, so creating a classroom culture that encourages questions relies heavily on positive praise. We jump for joy when our students ask a clear and meaningful mathematical question. The excitement may be a bit over the top, but it is a huge motivator for all your students to ask questions. We make sure that we are specifically praising the questions and not the answers: "I love how ______ asked ______ because it lets us ______." Then we soon hear students repeating those same questions in future lessons. When a student asks us a question while working with us one-on-one, we often say, "What a great question! Can we ask that to the class?" You can also create a public record of the mathematical questions the kids ask. After praising a student for asking a question, say, "Can we write that down so we remember to use it again?" Be sure to use and refer to the chart often so that students begin using it on their own.

When Things Don't Seem to Be Working

What do I do when my students are stating comments instead of asking questions?

We are always asking our kids to give compliments or suggestions when it comes to writer's workshops or other content areas, so it can be difficult to get kids to focus on questions when we have them share their math thinking. We find that it helps to review the difference between a question and a statement throughout the school year using the question/statement T-chart we discussed earlier in this chapter.

With primary students, it can also be helpful to have them think about how their voices sound when asking a question. When reading through your T-charts, have them practice raising their voices at the ends of their questions. They can also practice listening to a partner and determining if they are asking a question or making a statement.

Trying other physical sorting activities with questions and statements can also help students see the difference between questions and statements. One fun activity is a body sort. The teacher reads one question or statement at a time, and the students must move to one side of the room or the other to show which type of sentence they think it is.

What should I do when a student doesn't question?

There may be students in your class who are not comfortable asking questions, so it's crucial that you work on creating a classroom environment that promotes questioning. Providing turn and talk time before opening up questions to the whole group can often help shy or fearful students (as well as those who may be language learners or have language production challenges) gather their thoughts in a seemingly safer space. Try to pop around to students who usually hold off from asking something in the whole group. When you hear one of those students ask a question, or even an approximation of a question, get excited! When you feel the time is ready, ask them to share their question with the class. Encourage them to practice sharing their question with their partner again while the rest of the class finishes their discussions. It may take more time for certain students to ask questions, so we rely on talk moves such as rephrasing and repeating to help these students find their voices.

It is also important to be culturally aware of your students. In some cultures, it is considered inappropriate or impolite for children to ask questions of adults and others. In these cases, teachers should be deliberate in stating the purpose of questioning. Teachers can have direct conversations with these students to clarify the importance of asking questions at school to help our brains grow and learn.

When do I just tell?

Determining when to tell can be confusing within a student-centered math community, but we encourage you to avoid directly telling a student how to do something whenever possible. There will be times, however, when you do have to do some telling. One of those times is with mathematical conventions, symbols, or terms. For example, Mrs. Dance's class was able to prove that an equation was false. She used this opportunity to teach them the symbol for "is not equal." She showed them what the symbol was and gave the meaning. This is something that they would not have been able to come up with on their own. When teaching about a certain math convention, make sure it is relevant to a math concept that the kids have grappled with first. It is important that they have had time to work with the concept before you teach them about the convention. Other examples of mathematical conventions are symbols, specific vocabulary terms and mathematical properties, conventions such as order of operations, and units of standard measurement.

Just before sharing a convention with the class, make a big deal of it. "Listen up, mathematicians. I'm going to tell you something very important, and you know I never tell you *anything* in math." Kids look with gaping mouths and wide eyes. They know if you are telling, it must be important! In the end, we think it's best to err on the side of caution when thinking about when to tell, but a good clue is to ask yourself, "Is this something that the students could construct knowledge of on their own?" If the answer is no, then this may be an instance where telling is necessary.

Summary

In order for questions to be valuable tools that deepen student thinking and create new mathematical learning, they need to be intentional and purposeful. It takes a lot of time and patience to cultivate a classroom community of learners who embrace questions from the teacher as well as ask their own questions of each other. However, it is well worth the time investment, as it equips teachers with important assessment information and enables students to develop higher levels of understanding. Questions will help facilitate a mathematical discussion that promotes meaningful student discourse as children learn to question their own understanding and the assertions of their peers. You can develop this community of collaborative learners through teacher and student modeling, sentence stems, talk moves, and praise of focused mathematical questions. A room rich with questions is a recipe for developing deep, critical, and engaged mathematical thinkers.

Chapter Six Keeping Up the Momentum

It's easy, as we get wrapped up in the report card grading, parent-teacher conferences, curriculum materials, field trips, and the everyday demands of teaching, to let the effort it takes to maintain a positive classroom community slide. In order to implement the ideas in this book successfully, you as a teacher must keep them at the forefront of your mind and reinforce them to the point that they become common language in your classroom throughout the year. The more you reinforce each of the ideas presented in the chapters of this book with your students, the more they will value and reinforce them on their own.

In this chapter, we'll go over some quick tips and ideas that can keep the momentum going throughout the school year, even as our workload and stress load increase at pivotal points.

Invest the Time

At some point in our teaching careers, we've all learned the hard way that when we try to breeze over the teaching of classroom structures, routines, and expectations at the beginning of the year, we pay for it dearly in time spent correcting behaviors down the road. Alternatively, when we dedicate ample amounts of time at the beginning of the year to teaching behavior expectations, allowing students to practice those expectations and providing time for feedback and reflection, we vastly decrease the amount of time spent correcting behaviors down the road. The same is true when teaching the beliefs and values of a positive, inclusive mathematical community.

At the beginning of the year, it is essential to invest the time needed to help students truly understand the beliefs presented in this book. Taking time at the beginning of the year to teach many of the lessons suggested in this book will have huge payoffs throughout the year as you help your students develop a respectful community, common language around mathematical expectations, and awareness of their own mathematical confidence levels. Don't shortchange the amount of time spent to develop these ideals in your classroom.

You may also find at certain points throughout the year that you will need to reteach many of the ideas and expectations in this book. We can't expect our children to learn these ideas at the beginning of the year and then know them deeply without any check-ins along the way. It is important to be reflective as a teacher and notice when expectations are starting to slide a bit. Maybe a few students begin making some disrespectful comments, or a couple of children start doubting themselves as they struggle through problems. Instead of asking, "What is wrong with these children?" we need to ask, "What structure do I need to reteach and reinforce in order to get these kids back on track?" We must keep these beliefs alive in our classrooms throughout the year, not just at the beginning.

Finally, take advantage of the times when a new student joins your mathematical community. Embrace the chance to reteach some structures. You will soon find that your young mathematicians love to help teach and reinforce the beliefs with their new friends, which gives the new student more buy-in when they're learning from their peers rather than the teacher.

Keep It Student-Centered and Let Go!

Keeping our classrooms student-centered requires effort, explicit instruction of structures, and a release of control on the part of the teacher. Keeping control—telling students what to do and how to do it—often seems a lot easier than letting students guide their own learning. Releasing that control can be one of the most challenging tasks we face as teachers. However, we know that when students are able to take control of their own learning and construct understanding on their own, they learn new ideas more deeply and those ideas are more likely to stay with them over time.

Take moments throughout your year to reflect on your own instruction. It can help to videotape or have an instructional coach or colleague come in to observe a lesson. Keep track of how often students are asking questions and how often the teacher is delivering information. Reflect on who is doing most of the work, the students or the teacher? Practice asking questions instead of giving information. Whenever you are tempted to tell a student something, ask a question instead. Even the most skillful teachers slip into teacher-centered instruction, and while there is a time and place for this type of instruction, we must be reflective enough to realize when it's time to refocus the classroom on the students instead of the teacher.

Maintain a Growth Mindset

Whenever we set out to change something or try something new in our classrooms, it can feel messy and difficult. One of our favorite quotes to share with teachers as they begin the hard task of changing instruction is, "It is impossible to get better and look good at the same time" (Cameron 2016, 30). As we begin introducing these beliefs into our classrooms at the beginning of the year, things do not always progress as smoothly as we imagine they might. Students tear up as they make mistakes. They don't know what to say when it's their turn to share. Sometimes when you turn to the group and ask for questions, a hush falls over the group. Be sure to reflect on your own mindset in these moments. Just because it isn't working right now doesn't mean that you are on the wrong path or doing something wrong. During your next planning session, think about steps you can take to overcome the challenges you are facing. Look back through the chapters of this book and focus on the "When Things Don't Seem to Be Working" sections. Make steps that encourage growth instead of giving up because it seems hard.

One of the best ways to stay positive about the process of classroom change is to team up with your colleagues. They can be some of your greatest sources of inspiration and ideas as you tackle a change in your instructional practices. Whether they have already implemented this type of change or are doing it right along with you, the value of discussing challenges with colleagues is immeasurable as you connect over shared struggles and problem-solve together. Work with your team to engage in professional development opportunities that focus on these ideas about math instruction. Create common instructional goals together and support each other in achieving these goals.

As you work on maintaining and fostering your own growth mindset, be sure to keep these ideas alive with your students as well. When you make a mistake or something doesn't work out perfectly in a lesson, acknowledge this challenge with your students. Let them see you struggle and persevere the same way you are asking them to struggle and persevere with their mathematical learning. Keep posters and anchor charts up on your walls that encourage a positive mathematical mindset and refer to them often with your students. Make growth-mindset messages a common language in your classroom by deliberately using the terms yourself and by acknowledging and praising students when you hear them using growth-mindset messages with one another. It is one thing to introduce the idea to your students, but it is another thing completely when you make the idea live, grow, and breathe in your classroom.

Set One Goal at a Time and Be Deliberate

As you begin implementing some of the lessons and ideas from this book, the change can often feel overwhelming. Make a plan for yourself that is realistic and achievable. The best way to do this is to set one goal at a time. It is nearly impossible to change everything at once, and if you try to, the likelihood of successfully creating the community you want in your classroom decreases.

Choose one chapter or one idea within a chapter to be your focus for a set period of time. Write your goal in your plan book. Make sticky notes to put on a clipboard or near your gathering area. List out the questions you want to remember to ask, and place these on sticky notes or whatever works best for you. Choose the phrases and language you want your students to use with one another, and be deliberate in modeling that language. If you want students to begin justifying their thinking, don't ask them to "explain"—ask them to "justify." If you want them to question one another with partners, use the sentence stems you've provided in your own conversations throughout the day. The more deliberate you are about modeling and embodying the values you are trying to reinforce with your students, the more habitual these practices will become for everyone in the classroom.

Celebrate Successes

Finally, don't forget to celebrate your own successes and those of your students. It is far too easy to get caught up in the vision of where you want your classroom to be and forget how far you've come. Teachers, as natural perfectionists, tend to focus on what *isn't* working more often than on what *is*. Find moments throughout your day when you can acknowledge your students' growth.

We all know that making changes in our instruction can be hard. However, we must accept the responsibility we have to be the best teachers we can be for our students. For too long, we've been teaching math to students in a way that doesn't allow them the chance to develop deep understanding and make connections between mathematics and their lives. Once you begin shifting your math instruction, you will see the drastic changes in your students' attitudes toward math, and all the hard work will pay off in the end. We hope you enjoy the process of creating a classroom community based on beliefs that support true mathematical learning!

Appendix A

Math Attitude Survey

When I don't know what to do in math, I keep trying.	Yes	Sometimes	No
I share my thinking with others in math.	Yes	Sometimes	No
Math can be done in different ways.	Yes	Sometimes	No
I use math only at school.	Yes	Sometimes	No
I like math.	Yes	Sometimes	No
I can be good at math.	Yes	Sometimes	No
I talk to others in class about my ideas to solve math problems.	Yes	Sometimes	No

To download full-size versions of the appendices, please visit **http://hein.pub/ThinkingTogether** and click on the *Companion Resources* tab.

Appendix B

Problem-Solving Planning Template

Three-part lesson format

LESSON:

LEARNING TARGET:

PREREQUISITE SKILLS:

MATERIALS:

TASK:

BEFORE (LAUNCH)

ANTICIPATED MISCONCEPTIONS TO BE ADDRESSED:

VOCABULARY CHALLENGES IN THE TASK:

KEY QUESTIONS:

DURING (LAUNCH)

GROUPING (INDEPENDENT, PARTNER, OR SMALL GROUP):

KEY QUESTIONS:

PREPARATION FOR SHARING (STRATEGIES AND COMMON MISCONCEPTIONS TO LOOK FOR)

ENRICHMENT:

AFTER (LAUNCH)

SHARING ORDER:

KEY VOCABULARY TO TEACH:

KEY QUESTIONS:

Appendix C

Problem-Solving Planning Template with Guiding Questions

Three-part lesson format

LESSON:

- What lesson are you teaching?

LEARNING TARGET:

- Which Common Core State Standard does this lesson address?

PREREQUISITE SKILLS:

- What skills have you already taught that support new learning in this lesson?
- What skills have students learned in previous grades that support new learning in this lesson?

MATERIALS:

- What tools or resources will students need to give them entry to, and help them reason through, the activity?

TASK:

What is the problem task or main activity that students will be working on?

BEFORE (LAUNCH)

ANTICIPATED MISCONCEPTIONS TO BE ADDRESSED:

- What might the students struggle to understand in the task that will keep them from accessing the intended productive struggle of the problem?
- What can you do to help students understand the task (visualize, act it out, etc.)?

VOCABULARY CHALLENGES IN THE TASK:

- What vocabulary might students be unfamiliar with?
- How can you address any issues your ELLs may have with the vocabulary in the task?

KEY QUESTIONS:

- What questions can you ask students to ensure they understand what is known in the problem?
- What questions can you ask students to ensure they understand what they need to find out in the problem?
- What questions can you ask to formatively assess for student understanding of the problem?

DURING (LAUNCH)

GROUPING (INDEPENDENT, PARTNER, OR SMALL GROUP):

- How will students work on the task?
- How will you ensure students have a chance to talk about their thinking and understanding?

KEY QUESTIONS:

- What questions can you ask students who are struggling to get started?
- What questions can you ask students who solve the problem right away?
- What questions can you ask students to encourage them to justify their answer and model their thinking?
- What questions can you ask students who are having trouble working with a partner or group?

PREPARATION FOR SHARING (STRATEGIES AND COMMON MISCONCEPTIONS TO LOOK FOR)

- What strategies do you expect to see?
- What common misconceptions do you expect students to have?
- Which strategies might you have students share?

ENRICHMENT:

- What challenge will you provide for your students who need enrichment (e.g., challenge numbers, try another strategy)?

AFTER (LAUNCH)

SHARING ORDER:

- In what order would you like strategies to be shared?
- Why?

KEY VOCABULARY TO TEACH:

- What new mathematical vocabulary should be taught during the share?
- What mathematical vocabulary should be reviewed or reinforced during the share?

KEY QUESTIONS:

- What specific questions will you ask to help students make sense of the mathematical ideas they are expected to learn and make connections among the different strategies or solutions presented?
- What questions will you ask to help students explain their thinking?
- What questions will you ask to keep students focused on the learning target?

Recommended Resources

Read-Alouds for Teaching Respect

Chrysanthemum, Kevin Henkes

Hooway for Wodney Wat, Helen Lester

How Full Is Your Bucket?, Tom Rath and Mary Reckmeyer

The Invisible Boy, Trudy Ludwig

Lacey Walker, Nonstop Talker, Christianne Jones

Miss Nelson Is Missing!, Harry Allard

Yoko, Rosemary Wells

Read-Alouds and Websites for Encouraging Confidence

Beautiful Oops!, Barney Saltzberg

The Girl Who Never Made Mistakes, Mark Pett and Gary Rubinstein

Koala Lou, Mem Fox

Leo the Late Bloomer, Robert Kraus

The Little Engine That Could, Watty Piper

The Most Magnificent Thing!, Ashley Spires

Snowflake Bentley, Jacqueline Briggs Martin

What Do You Do with a Problem?, Kobi Yamada

Your Fantastic Elastic Brain, JoAnn Deak

www.youcubed.org

https://ideas.classdojo.com

http://trainugly.com/growth-mindset-hub

Read-Alouds for Thinking Differently

The Dot and *Ish*, Peter H. Reynolds

Froodle, Antoinette Portis

Going Places, Peter H. Reynolds and Paul Reynolds

Rosie Revere, Engineer, Andrea Beaty

What Do You Do with an Idea?, Kobi Yamada

Instructional Support Resources for Teachers

5 Practices for Orchestrating Productive Mathematics Discussions, Margaret S. Smith and Mary Kay Stein

Accessible Mathematics, Steven Leinwand

Children's Mathematics: Cognitively Guided Instruction, Thomas P. Carpenter, Elizabeth Fennema, Megan Loef Franke, Linda Levi, and Susan B. Empson

Classroom Discussions: Using Math Talk to Help Students Learn, Suzanne H. Chapin, Catherine O'Connor, and Nancy Canavan Anderson

Intentional Talk: How to Structure and Lead Productive Mathematical Discussions, Elham Kazemi and Allison Hintz

Mathematical Mindsets, Jo Boaler

Mindset: The New Psychology of Success, Carol S. Dweck

Principles to Actions: Ensuring Mathematical Success for All, NCTM

Smarter Together! Collaboration and Equity in the Elementary Math Classroom, NCTM

Teaching Student-Centered Mathematics: Developmentally Appropriate Instruction for Grades Pre-K–2, John A. Van de Walle, LouAnn H. Lovin, Karen S. Karp, and Jennifer M. Bay-Williams

Teaching Student-Centered Mathematics: Developmentally Appropriate Instruction for Grades 3–5, John A. Van de Walle, Karen S. Karp, LouAnn H. Lovin, and Jennifer M. Bay-Williams

Thinking Mathematically: Integrating Arithmetic and Algebra in Elementary School, Thomas P. Carpenter, Megan Loef Franke, and Linda Levi

Young Mathematicians at Work: Constructing Number Sense, Addition, and Subtraction, Catherine Twomey Fosnot and Maarten Dolk (and others in this series)

References

Boaler, Jo. 2016. *Mathematical Mindsets: Unleashing Students' Potential Through Creative Math, Inspiring Messages and Innovative Teaching*. San Francisco: Jossey-Bass.

Cameron, Julia. 2016. *The Artist's Way: A Spiritual Path to Higher Creativity*. New York: TarcherPerigree.

CCSSO (Council of Chief State School Officers). 2010. *Common Core State Standards*. http://corestandards.org.

Danielson, Charlotte. 2014. *The Framework for Teaching: Evaluation Instrument*. www.danielsongroup.org.

Dweck, Carol S. 2006. *Mindset: The New Psychology of Success*. New York: Ballantine.

———. 2007. "The Perils and Promises of Praise." *Educational Leadership* 65: 34–39.

———. 2014. "The Power of Believing That You Can Improve." TEDxNorrköping. www.ted.com/talks/carol_dweck_the_power_of_believing_that_you_can_improve.

Katz, Lillian G. 1993. "Dispositions: Definitions and Implications of Early Childhood Practices." In *Perspectives from ERICIEECE: A Monograph Series, No. 4*. Urbana, IL: ERIC Clearinghouse on Elementary and Early Childhood Education.

The Math Forum at NCTM. 2017. "Notice and Wonder." http://mathforum.org/pow/noticewonder/.

Meyer, Dan. 2010. "Math Class Needs a Makeover." TEDxNYED. March. www.ted.com/talks/dan_meyer_math_curriculum_makeover.

National Council of Teachers of Mathematics (NCTM). 2014. *Principles to Actions: Ensuring Mathematical Success for All.* Reston, VA: National Council of Teachers of Mathematics.

Ray-Riek, Max. 2016. "Teacher Appreciation: Max Ray-Riek on a Fifth-Grade Math Teacher." Heinemann blog video, 3:15. Posted May 4, 2016. http://www.heinemann.com/blog/taw-max-ray-riek-5-4/.

Van de Walle, John A., LouAnn H. Lovin, Karen S. Karp, and Jennifer M. Bay-Williams. 2014. *Teaching Student-Centered Mathematics: Developmentally Appropriate Instruction for Grades Pre-K–2.* 2nd ed. Boston: Pearson.